To my late husband Peter, for his friendship, unending support, good sense and generous listening.

To our four daughters, Barbara, Geraldine, Clare and Monica, who have loved me and who help me to understand so much more.

To the hundreds of children all over the country who have confided in me and shared with me.

And to parents, teachers and special friends who have trusted and encouraged me for thirty years in this work.

CONTENTS

INTRODUCTION

Adolescence is the time between the ages of 10 and 18 when your thinking, your feelings and your body are changing. Sometimes you may imagine that everybody except you has all the answers to life. But, be assured, most other adolescents are searching for answers, just as you are.

The purpose of this new edition of *Ready, Steady, Grow!* is to help you to understand better the many ins and outs of development from childhood to adulthood. It is written especially for ten- to thirteen-year-olds as they grow into the new century. You will be amongst the first teenagers of the century – the trend-setters of the future! May it be blessed.

I want you to be happy and excited about this stage in your life. It is such a challenge. I hope that you will be able to discuss the things that you read here with a parent, teacher or friend.

This book is also for the adults who are trying to help and understand you. No-one has all the answers but it's great to have people around you who will listen to the questions so that you can get to know each other in a deeper way. Together you can work out the plans for the building of YOU.

So – On your marks – Ready, Steady, Grow!

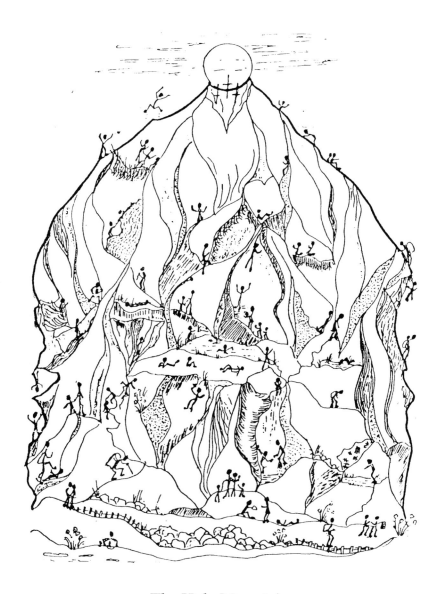

The Holy Mountain
Our Life Journey

CHAPTER 1

BUILDING YOURSELF

Growing up is like building a house. You don't begin by making a roof. There has to be a plan. You have to put down firm foundations. You are the architect and you are going to plan what kind of person you want to become.

Be patient about the plan. Think well as you put down the foundations. Ask yourself questions:

- What kind of person do I want to become?
- What gifts and talents do I have?
- What qualities and characteristics do I admire in other people?
- What unique contribution might I make?
- What goals do I believe to be good?

For example: I am deeply and personally convinced that LOVE is the most important value in life. I want love to be the strong foundation on which I build my life. After all, everyone needs love. (Don't you?) Love brings peace.

There are different kinds of love:

Love of God, love of myself
Love of family, love of neighbours
Love of friends and sexual love

I want to understand each of these different loves better so that I can learn to make people feel worthwhile, happy, respected and appreciated.

That's a tall order, a life challenge. Having decided to face up to the challenge, I must then ask myself a basic question about whatever I'm planning to do, write or say.

> Is this the loving thing to do?

Some people regard power or wealth or fashion or fun as the most important things in their lives. They keep wondering 'How can I make more money out of what I'm planning to do?' or 'Will I become more powerful if I do this?'. Power, wealth, fashion and fun are normal human desires. But they need to be directed by love. Love keeps our ambitions gentle and kind and prevents us getting greedy or climbing over other people, hurting them as we try to reach the top.

CHAPTER 2

WHAT IS LIFE FOR?

We each have to ask ourselves what life is for when we set about deciding how we want to live. The Christian believes that life is the testing time during which we *freely choose* to work our way closer to God, contributing our very best to keep the world as beautiful as God made it. If we try to do that then death is just a step across the horizon to the reward that God has promised.

> 'Eye has not seen, nor ear heard, nor has it entered into the minds of men and women what God has prepared for those who love him.' *1 Cor 2:9*

I believe that the only things worth doing are the things God wants me to do. And these are the things that make for peace and happiness.

'God is Love'

That's what St John told us. Choosing love as the headline in your life means that every time you bring love to another person, you bring God to them. God has left us free to choose to bring him (love) into the world. Teresa of Ávila was surely thinking of this when she wrote:

> 'Christ has no body now on earth but yours,
> no hands but yours, no feet but yours.
> Yours are the eyes with which his love
> looks out to the world;
> yours are the feet with which he goes
> about doing good;
> yours are the hands with which he blesses
> people now.' *St Teresa of Ávila*

So that's the challenge of being Christian; to be other Christs. Take it on quite simply as the project of your life. Just open your hands to accept the help and gifts God will give you. When we are uncomplicated and childlike in our love and acceptance of God as our 'Abba' (the loving, familiar name Jesus called his father – it means 'Daddy'), he bends down and whispers his secret in our ear. The brilliant scientist Einstein wrote:

> 'The final answer to the 'Why' of the universe has to be simple and beautiful.'

Sometimes it seems too hard and too much trouble. Maybe we'll be left out of the fun and games if we want to include someone the others don't like or if we stop to console someone who has been rejected. Perhaps people will laugh at us if we share our lunch with someone who told tales and is now alone?

Are you the only one?
God wants sad, rejected, hurt and lonely people to experience his love. Maybe you are the only one who will

bring his message at a particular time. It often takes courage to love. It takes a great deal of practice.

You may ask 'How can I love a person who has been mean to me or let me down, or is just unattractive to me?' Of course we cannot feel love for everyone but we can wish them well. We can make the decision to forgive, to try to understand, to smile and to reach out a helping hand.

That decision must be freely made by you.

> *People* judge one another by looking at appearances. *God* judges us by looking at our hearts.

CHAPTER 3

FOLLOW YOUR LEADER

No-one can decide that they want to be like Christ and to choose him as their leader unless they first ask what kind of a man he was. Do the gospels show him as a person we can admire and wish to copy?

Well, we are told that he was strong, forgiving, understanding. He healed the sick. He must have had a warm, smiling personality because children crowded around him – children don't go for dour, unhappy people. He was able to fish and climb and walk for hours in every kind of weather. His charm, strength of character and the attractiveness of his message drew thousands to hear him – and that was when there was no advertising, no TV, no radio or newspapers to promote and aid him.

Numbers of women felt great love for him and he for them. Men downed their tools and followed him. He didn't water down the truth in order to make himself popular. Even as he died he asked his father to forgive those who crucified him.

Three days after his death he had his greatest triumph. He rose from the dead and proved to us that death is not the end. There is a glorious life afterwards.

> 'Nothing will separate us from the love of God demonstrated by Jesus Christ.'

The Bread of Life

So, is Christ the kind of leader you find challenging enough to follow? The fact that he makes himself available to us under the appearance of bread and wine makes it possible for us to be strengthened regularly. 'Whoever eats this bread will live forever.' Christ has promised. In every Holy Communion he becomes part of you and me. In this way love becomes part of us. It is like being refuelled with love and being free to let that love flow out to others. The choice is ours.

God also wants us to love ourselves – he created each of us as unique and gifted. He wants us to have fun and joy, to laugh and spread happiness. In these ways we share in the very nature of God.

CHAPTER 4

LOVE IS...

An Exercise: Ingredients of Love

> **Love is...** Kind, caring, forgiving, fun, patient, loyal, understanding, trustworthy, gentle, fair, honest, respectful, listening, unselfish, sharing, generous, sympathetic, encouraging, helpful, smiling, agreeable, warm and truthful.

Now substitute the words 'Jesus is...' for 'Love is...' (Jesus is kind, Jesus is caring, etc.).

Then substitute the words 'I am...' (I am kind, I am caring, etc.).

It would be impossible for a human being to have all those virtues together. However, make a mental note of the qualities you are pleased to have and those you would like to improve. (There is no need to announce your personal decisions to anyone.)

Friendship

When you note the 'ingredients of love' (above) you realise that these include the qualities we would all like to find in friendship. Do you offer these qualities to your friends or to your family members? Strange, isn't it, how mean, teasing, rude, hurtful, bitchy and unhelpful some people are to their very own families? Can you think why this might be? Can you do anything to make your home an even happier place than it is?

Do you think it would be important to find the qualities listed above in a friend of the opposite sex? ('Sex' just means the difference between men and women).

Is it normal to have pals of the opposite sex without actually 'going with' that person? It should be considered quite normal.

But sometimes girls and boys tease one another about 'going with' someone when they may be only friendly neighbours. This teasing is embarrassing and spoils a perfectly ordinary boy/girl friendship. No one likes to be teased. But it would be a pity to end a neighbourly friendship just because some classmates stupidly tease you about it. Coolly explain that you are just pals (with this person of the opposite sex) and continue to behave quite normally with him or her. You don't have to fancy a person in order to stop on the road for a chat or walk to the shops together. There can be some jealousy in this kind of teasing. And it is old-fashioned.

> It is good to have plenty of casual friendships with both boys and girls.

It takes time and spadework to form a *deep* friendship in which you feel totally at ease, relaxed, completely yourself. It doesn't happen in just a week or two.

I'll be talking more about boy/girl friendships and 'going together' a bit further on. But first let's look at the questions in the next chapter.

CHAPTER 5

WHO AM I?

Making a list is a good way of discovering yourself. Have a look at yourself, both outside and inside. Ask yourself a few questions:

Am I a warm, comforting person?
Am I sensitive; a good manager?
Am I honest with myself?
Am I a good family person?
Am I fun to be with?
Do I think of other people's needs?
Do I know what I myself most need?
Am I a helper?
Am I creative?
Am I a dreamer or a doer – or both?
Do I tell a story well?
Am I calm and laid back?
Am I excitable and anxious?
Am I good at dancing, singing, making, mending, sport, art?

Have I good skin? (or can I put up with a few spots from time to time?)
Have I nice eyes? A good build? Good teeth? An open personality? A quiet nature?

Am I concerned for the aged, the ill, the rejected, children…?

AND SO VERY MANY OTHER POSSIBILITIES…

Write down all the things you see about yourself and this will give you a basic picture of yourself as a gifted human being who still has the possibility of developing even greater loveliness of personality and character.

There will be personality traits you want to improve. Just take one of these at a time, for example 'SMILE MORE'. Write that on a piece of sticky paper and stick it to your mirror. Then every time you look at your outside appearance, you can check on some particular aspect of your inside beauty too.

> Smile a while, and when you smile, another smiles. And then there are miles and miles of smiles.

Maturity means becoming able to make responsible decisions which take into account what is best and most loving (even though this is sometimes hard) for everyone concerned. The mature person has formed basic principles and firm values in life.

At your age you aren't fully mature yet because maturity necessitates the experience of years and the courage to build your unique life confidently and intelligently. But you are more mature now than when you were eight. Are you a better person now? Wiser? Wise people read and think and plan the next bit of life. Have you heard this:

> A sculptor succeeded after years in carving a magnificent horse. Someone asked him: 'How did you get it so perfect and lifelike?' He replied: 'Well, I just kept chipping away the bits that weren't 'horse'.'

So we keep chipping away the bits of ourselves that are not making us all that we could be. Maturity also means not taking yourself too seriously. We all make mistakes. Learn from them.

We've all struggled with shyness and made foolish comments at times. Don't pretend to be anything that you are not. Leave other people free to travel the path they have chosen while sticking to your chosen path as best you can. You may need to change some plans as life develops and you see some things differently. Forgive yourself when you go wrong – we all do.

What others want you to be
Don't try to live up to all the expectations of other people. Even what you wear should be what you like. People will want all sorts of things from you – some good, some bad. You will be both criticised and praised at different times. But your okay-ness doesn't depend on what others think of you. Just be the best 'YOU' you know how to be, the unique person God created you to be.

Have you heard of the experiment done with caterpillars?

In the centre of a large saucer was placed some tasty greenery. All around the edge of the saucer thirty caterpillars were placed head to tail. They started walking, each following the one in front. Even though they became tired and hungry, not one of them wanted to break out of the procession. In a few hours one or two grew weak or died and fell off the saucer-edge. The others continued processing until only two were left. One of those saw the greens in the centre of the saucer and climbed wearily down the slope to eat. The other followed. These were the two that became mature and beautiful.

Are you able to break away from the crowd and do the different thing? Discuss what that might be.

CHAPTER 6

WHAT IS A FRIEND?

Friendship with your own sex
Young people, girls particularly, tend to be possessive in friendship. They want to own their best friend, to keep her for themselves, not allow her to have other friends. They feel jealous if they see her chatting or having fun with someone else.

But we all need more than one friend. Each friend is unique and unrepeatable and contributes something special to our lives – the quiet, gentle, listening friend, the talkative, funny one, the sporty one who encourages us to walk, swim and run, the brainy one…. It is not true friendship to deny your pal friendship with others.

Putting your friend in a cage
But you may feel jealous if you see your friend with another mate. You may feel that she or he cares less about

you. You may want to put your friend in a cage and keep her or him for yourself.

We cannot imprison the human spirit
True friendship leaves the friend free and trusted. We can all experience friendship with a variety of people of whom no two are the same. So your friend may have other pals, but no other one will be exactly like you. Discuss other friends, learn about them, be open and trusting. Never deceive or lie to one another. Holding onto a friend possessively is like a hunter tying a fox to a tree. That completely spoils the hunt!

Let me give you an example:

Sue and Eva are in the same class and live quite close to one another. They are great friends. Sue goes to swimming lessons regularly and Eva collects tapes and CDs and learns the guitar.

At swimming Sue meets Sharon and Tricia. They occasionally go to town together or have chips on the way home.

Eva has a cousin who is music-mad so she goes to concerts with him. She is particularly pally with one girl, Nan, who is super on the guitar.

With these different interests, can Sue and Eva still be friends? Of course they can! Now when they meet they have more to chat about because they have met with other friends in the meantime. Sometimes they all meet in the park. Sue asks Eva about the latest gig and about the posters around her bedroom. Eva goes to swimming competitions and mixes with Sue's swimming friends. They still feel close to one another and *trust one another.*

So a few friendships can exist simultaneously unless jealousy and possessiveness spoil it all. Not all friendships last for ever. People change their interests, go to different schools, move house. But there is never a reason for dropping an old friend in a way that hurts that person. Can't they still meet now and again and discuss honestly with one another what is happening in their lives? At your age people grow up at different rates, their interests move on so a friendship can drift. Just remember – no hurting of the old pal. Try to understand what is happening and keep a thread of the old relationship going. Avoid, in your disappointment, the temptation to talk bitchily about this other person. That won't endear you to anyone. People will listen to your unkind gossip but won't be attracted to you.

All friends, including adults, have rows and differences from time to time. It's important to listen patiently to one another and try to understand. Be ready to forgive and to agree to differ.

Do you think God is pleased when people whisper mean, unkind and untrue gossip about mates? Well, answer that question for yourself!

Nowadays boys understand friendship in a deeper way than they did long ago. They are well able to see the point in the example given above and to describe how it would be if the friendship were between boys.

There are stories for role play and discussion on pp. 113-119. Try them in your group.

CHAPTER 7

WHAT SHOULD I DO?

Choices and decisions

At adolescence you are naturally beginning to feel the need to be free to make some choices and decisions for yourself. But no one is ever totally independent. Whatever one person does always has some effect on someone else – or even on an entire community.

```
'No person is an island.'
```

We need and depend on one another in all kinds of ways.

There are times when you like the security of having your parents in the background. Don't bawl at them when they try to make suggestions or offer opinions. While you are rightly seeking new freedoms do try to discuss what you want calmly. Let them explain their point of view just as you would like to be listened to by them. Reach sensible decisions together.

Spare a thought for your parents who understand that you are beginning to want more freedom. They may be afraid to allow too much in case, in your natural inexperience, you hurt yourself. There can be misunderstandings and mistakes on both sides.

If someone tells you something personal that is very private and secret NEVER tell anyone else. Be trustworthy. But if you consider it to be something bad or wrong confide in a parent or teacher.

It's time for dialogue – What's that?

- Tell each other what you truly feel and why.
- Listen patiently to each other, not only with the ears but with the heart.
- Get a feel for the other person's life situation, responsibilities and concerns.
- Dialogue is not argument; it is caring discussion.
- Dialogue is a vital part of all relationships.
- Learn dialogue now: it's a valuable ability.

In dialogue we respect the other person, recognising his or her right to their feelings. We listen attentively, then we express our point of view with as much truth and gentleness as we can. It is a good idea to allow for short silences when dialogue is going on, to allow what is being said to sink in. So, count to ten before you jump in with your responses.

So often in conversation neither person really listens to the other with respect. Practise this kind of listening at home and with friends. Explain to your parents how you understand the notion of 'dialogue', so that the very mention of the word prepares the family for a really loving exchange of deeply-felt needs, opinions and ideas.

CHAPTER 8

THE SEE-SAW OF LIFE

Puberty is the stage when your body starts developing from that of a child into that of an adult. It all happens gradually and gently. Girls may begin puberty at about the age of ten and are usually fully developed by sixteen. Boys begin at about twelve and are fully developed by seventeen. All the time your body is developing you are also maturing in your knowledge, thinking and making decisions about your life. No two people mature at exactly the same rate. It is much more interesting that we have our differences rather than being mass-produced like identical rails of jumpers in a chain store!

Adolescence simply refers to the years between childhood and adulthood. So adolescence is approximately the ten years between the ages of ten and twenty. It includes the psychological, intellectual, emotional, spiritual and physical growing up. (The word adolescence comes from a Latin word which means to grow up). It is the most natural thing in the world to be interested in how your intellect and your body develop.

The ups and downs
Moods. Because of all the bodily changes it is normal to feel a bit 'down' some days and happier on other days. It may be simply to do with the weather, or it may be a deeper upset or a fantastic surprise. Some good happening can lift us out of 'the blues' in an instant.

In adolescence and in the teen years feelings become more intense and may swing up and down a bit more often. You may sometimes feel cranky or touchy or 'fed-up' for no apparent reason. These mood swings are often due to chemical changes taking place in your developing body.

All this will settle down in time. Meanwhile you can help yourself enormously by taking control of your moods. Don't just slouch in the most comfortable chair in front of the television, glaring at anyone who comes near you. Distract yourself from the mood, get up and do something you really like doing. Keep away from anyone or any situation that really irritates you. Go for a walk or a cycle or kick a ball with a pal (it's a lot better than kicking your little brother who kicks back – and then…!). Do something to help someone.

It's great to become aware that you are able to beat those 'blues'. If you have worries think them out one by one. Explain them to a parent or friend.

Sometimes, if mum (or dad) is too busy to listen, you imagine that you are not loved. So you settle in to a great wallow of self-pity.

Perhaps your parents are tired or over-worked or stressed-out at just the same time as you have a 'down' mood. Maybe they give out to you because you are grouchy,

cheeky, making trouble with a brother or sister, untidy, late for meals or generally unhelpful. Parents are human too. Isn't it understandable that they don't like such behaviour? But they still love you. It's like when a baby cries all night, every night. No one likes the crying (the *behaviour*), but everyone still loves the baby.

A baby doesn't yet know how to control itself. But you are *learning to master your ups and downs of mood.* You are beginning to understand, too, that there is always blue sky behind the clouds. We must all be big enough to say: 'Sorry I was mad at you' and then begin the journey to understanding. Feeling 'fed-up' is something we all experience. The greater the person the stronger he or she will become at mastering moods.

Anger is not a bad thing in itself. Letting off steam can be a healthy reaction at the right time. But we cannot spend our lives like three-year-olds who kick and scream every time they don't get their own way. We have to learn to express anger fairly and appropriately. Remember how angry Christ was with the money-lenders who used the temple for their business transactions? That was *appropriate anger*. It would be emotionally unhealthy always to pretend to agree and yet be raging inwardly. It is wise to express anger in some way – perhaps to the person or people concerned or to a sympathetic friend. Even to thump your pillow gets rid of some of our angry energy. To share intense feelings helps us come to terms with them. A walk, run, cycle or climb out in the open is a great help in recovering your calm.

Sometimes people show aggression and rudeness at home with the family when, in another person's house, they would be kind and well-mannered. I wonder why we are sometimes so ready to let loose our horrible selves at home, rejecting and hurting the people who are closest to us? (Discuss.)

CHAPTER 9

WHY HAVE MANNERS?

Are good manners to be encouraged?

Good manners are part of loving. They include:

- opening a door for someone
- carrying a tray
- giving up the cosy chair near the fire
- helping someone on with their coat
- turning down the volume when someone is tired
- listening to an old person with respect
- being punctual

Why do some people think that these gracious and caring gestures are uncool and old-fashioned? Perhaps because they haven't thought out the meaning behind the gesture. Have you thought it out? We form our character and our values by thinking out such things and deciding if we have a feeling for the truth that is at the heart of the value. 'But', you say, 'people might jeer me for doing those things'. Yes, indeed they might. So what are you going to do? Are you going to be like the caterpillar doing what everyone else does, afraid to do the good or wise thing that your own heart tells you to do? The choice to grow up and be true to yourself is yours.

What are the values in the kindly gestures listed here as 'Good Manners'?

Facing those rules
There will always be rules for all of us to live by. Rules are

most often made to safeguard us rather than to imprison us. We obey the traffic lights, we observe the double yellow lines, we accept the rules of any club we join. If we think the rules at home, in the club or wherever, are wrong, then we should think out alternative approaches and express them calmly and clearly to the authority concerned, whether it be a politician, a teacher, a parent, a club leader or a parking authority. Shouting, banging doors, name-calling, cursing or just flouting the particular rule indicates a person's immaturity. (Indeed, not all middle-aged people behave in a mature way in the face of authority or differing opinion!)

Your viewpoint

You may have a very original viewpoint which, expressed well, will change the rule. Or your view may change when the other person has quietly and clearly explained the 'why' of the rule. It is immature to be unwilling to change or to refuse to admit that you were mistaken. It's great to be able to say: 'You're right. I'm sorry'. Parents, too, have to apologise at times.

CHAPTER 10

WHY HAVE A CHURCH?

Rejecting the Church

> Some people seem to consider it cool and liberated to reject the Church unthinkingly. Some say that we can be loving and good without a Church. Let's think about that.

Remember when we looked at the person of Christ (pp. 14-15). We decided that he was a man of integrity worthy of admiration, a man who spoke the truth and lived it. I'm sure you agree with the main message he preached: love, peace, justice, forgiveness, concern for the poor and underprivileged. He also told us that he and the Father are one. So we know that God translated God into human terms in Jesus Christ so that we would know about life, death and resurrection. (I write 'him' for God. But God is *parent* – mother and father.)

Christ knew that no one person on their own can bring messages of vital importance and truth to the whole world. So he formed a group of normal people, to help him. Nothing unusual about that. After all, no one person with a political ideal remains alone when trying to promote the ideal. Such a person forms a political party, a group of people who will help to spread the message. This is also the case with organisations like Live Aid or the St Vincent de Paul Society or Friends of the Earth. There must be a large group of people who study their objectives, work together, set up the rules of the organisation and plan how to further its aims. Every so often they meet to share the results, learn from one another's experience and hear what the chairperson or director has to say. Thus they are encouraged and refuelled to set out again.

Christ's group
The group Christ formed is the Christian Church. Neither you nor I could bring its message far enough on our own. We need the support of the group, giving us courage and affirming us. Some topics that arise do not find agreement with everyone. Every so often (particularly on Sundays) we meet together to hear the leader's words and feel at one with this vast army of followers all striving, in our human way, to live out the message. We are encouraged and strengthened by receiving the Bread of Life and hearing Jesus' words: 'Whoever eats this bread will live forever'.

The promotion of Christian love is not easy in a pleasure-seeking, warring world. We need one another's support. We are all weak and human so we try to pool our strengths and back each other up in order to spread the message of love.

Do your best with the teachings you find difficult. Have the humility to ask God for greater insight into his truths. Church leaders are human like the rest of us. They make mistakes and have to keep trying all the time to 'get it right' for the people of our time. So have the compassion of Christ for them. And do some deep thinking for yourself.

Give God Time
We also need the peace and reassurance which God will give us when we spend time alone with him. Whatever worries you have about growing up, about boyfriends and girlfriends and parents and exams – God knows about

them all. He has said: 'I have called you by your name…
You are mine!' (Isaiah 43). Even the hairs on your head are
numbered.

So be still and wait on God for even two minutes a day. Just
relax, be quiet, let your body go quite limp – like a rag doll
– and breathe deeply, evenly, naturally. Sit like this in a
place that is peace-inducing and quiet. Perhaps have a
candle burning as you let his comforting words sink into
the core of your being: 'You are precious in my eyes' he has
said 'And I love you…' (Insert your own name where I
have put the dots. Because he is speaking to you.) Allow
his love to be realised in you. Distractions are
understandable, but don't grasp them, let them flow by

37

like leaves on a stream. Don't try to work out your problems during this quiet time. There is a Zen proverb:

> 'When the pupil is ready The Teacher will appear.'

God will be with you in a new and different way when you have a problem if you learn to simply relax with him. Don't give up because of distractions. If you give the few minutes faithfully and regularly you will grow to know and hear him. In your heart call him by his familiar names – 'Abba', 'Father', 'Jesus'. You will begin to increase the time you spend in such peace. Try it. It works! (see also pp. 120-121.)

CHAPTER 11

BEING YOUR OWN PERSON

C'mon, have a smoke!
Are you afraid of a jar?
Why don't you wear mod clothes?
Everyone 'gets off' with someone.
Discos are cool. You're such a creep!
Going to church again – Holy Joe?
C'mon, we're only lifting cheap stuff.
Take a whiff: it won't kill you.
Do you want to be in our gang or not?
Tell your parents you were studying.
Sod off! You're out of the last century.
Look at his hair! He's like his grand-da.
Let the fellas do it. It's cool.
A lick, teacher's pet. What a nerd!

Did you ever hear such pressurising comments? (Maybe you could think of some others to add to the list.)

Peer pressure means pressure from your own age group to do things that you may know to be wrong or that you may not feel ready to do yet – or that may be unwise, dishonest, hurtful, deceitful or, in some way, simply distasteful to you.

Peer pressure tries to push you to do or wear or say things that others do, wear and say.

It's not wrong if all the caterpillars wear green body-suits. But caterpillars are not intelligent or thoughtful or capable of making their minds up for themselves. Is it okay that someone doesn't like jeans, or doesn't have a clue about Man United, or hates discos? *Have they a right to be different from the gang?* Of course they have. Differences are interesting.

If you are being put under such pressure don't start a fight. Be cool and smiling when you say 'No' to the offer of a drink or when you don't want to go to a disco. Have the courage to do your own thing, be your own person. Don't get anxious, nervous, cross-looking or try to run away. STAY COOL. Ask them about the disco, tell them to feel free to do what they want just as you feel free to do what you want. Isn't that okay? Discuss it in class so that you share your views.

Assertiveness means being straight-forward, respectful, firm and honest in telling other people your needs and opinions. Supposing someone was trying to get you to smoke and you had decided that you would never do so. Quietly state what you believe to be the right thing to do. Explain your position. If the other person says 'Aw c'mon', smile, look the person in the eye and say, 'Chris, I don't ever intend to smoke.' Respect the other's right to have a different opinion. Don't be sarcastic. Listen to him/her/them. Keep in eye contact with Chris and keep your voice calm. Don't back away anxiously. If all the group are doing something you do not think is right (like messing a wall with graffiti), move off firmly with your head held high and a cool step – 'See you tomorrow'. If they laugh at you, do not turn around. Remember, some will secretly admire your courage.

Aggressive behaviour is quite different to assertive behaviour. The aggressive person shouts, argues, loses their temper, becomes hostile and bullying, and often hurts and angers someone they love, such as a parent or a good friend.

Finally, don't scuttle away like a frightened rabbit, or be so anxious that you try to please everyone. You'll never succeed in that. You have a right to your well thought-out opinion. Stick to it assertively and listen when others try to explain their viewpoint. There are times when another person may cause you to think more deeply, even to change your opinion. You may bring others to change also. That's how all of us learn.

> Role-play a scene in which a few people are rejecting the person who won't smoke (or drink or whatever). See how the situation can be worked out. Acting it out increases understanding.

Fear and Freedom

Fear can be a strong emotion in adolescence. There are many different fears:

- that you'll make a fool of yourself
- that other people won't like you
- that you'll be left out
- that you'll be smaller or taller or weaker than the others
- that your parents will be difficult
- that you'll never get a boyfriend or girlfriend

Suddenly you realise that you are not free at all. Perhaps you are a slave to doing what you think will make you popular. That's what so often leads people into life-destructive behaviour: drug-taking, alcohol abuse, sex abuse, violence, smoking, law-breaking, etc.

Rather than being smart, liberated forms of behaviour, these often point to weak people with a fear of saying 'No' when, deep down, they believe they should say 'No' and may actually want to.

So, learn to say 'No' in a pleasant, easy way, and be quite firm and non-defensive about it. You have a human right to be your unique self.

You have to be ready to think out the *values* behind what they want you do and the *consequences* of doing it. Maybe they want you to crash the traffic lights, to swim in a dark, unknown lake, to try a certain drug 'just for a laugh', to cheat or steal, to have sex or…. There are so many things you might be encouraged to do.

Even now, as you read this list, think about what you believe to be the right and caring and sensible thing to do in these situations. Then you'll be more ready with your response should the situation arise. If they say 'Everyone else does it', you can reply with a grin, 'Well, you've just met the one who doesn't'. Go off cheerfully without judging or name-calling. Maybe others will follow you. Secretly there are sure to be those who admire your courage to be different.

Exercise
Discuss the examples given above.

CHAPTER 12

BE AWARE – TAKE CARE!

Drinking, Driving, Drug Taking, Solvent Abuse, Smoking
The normal social drinking of a mature person is quite legitimate. Nevertheless, there are people who never take alcohol. That's okay too. What is not okay is the person who seeks courage in a bottle, who drinks alcohol (even when under-age) to seem to be smart and to look as though he or she has a great personality.

Many people, young and not so young, actually boast about being 'stoned' and 'legless' on alcohol or drugs. What is so great about not being able to control yourself or needing drink to make you imagine that you have personality? As you know, alcohol slows reactions and makes people irresponsible. Then there are dangers like:

- Road accidents
- Scandal-giving
- Unwanted pregnancy
- Wasting money
- Upsetting family life
- Failing at work
- Breakdown in relationships
- Health damage
- Job loss
- Failing exams
- Disappointment with self
- Going against God

(Discuss.)

In this country we are far too tolerant of people who drink excessively: wives, mothers and girlfriends should stop cleaning up the mess made by drunken men and tell them what they really think of them. Drunken women are regarded by many as pathetic and men often sneer at the degrading behaviour of girls who drink excessively – while encouraging them to 'have just one more'. Drunken people or even people who are merry – a bit tipsy and consequently uninhibited – are often abused by others.

Drugs – Do not be tempted to try any form of drug. Even one tablet of 'E' is a killer. Remember that every tortured addict started by 'trying just one'. The 'great sensation' people speak of can become hell on earth. Marijuana ('pot', 'hash' or 'grass') is not as harmless as some people claim. Recent studies have shown it to have delayed ill-effects on the brain and reproductive organs.

Driving is another danger for reckless teenagers. 'Joy-riding' is a poor name for the wrongful activity of stealing cars and often crashing them as result of irresponsible, untrained driving. No joy there!

It is quite understandable that teenagers want huge and overwhelmingly exciting experiences. But you've got to keep your wits about you. Some people look on cars and motorbikes as playthings and long to 'rev' up and roar around in them. Motorcycle accidents are on the increase. Brain damage is often the result for the pillion passenger and/or the driver. Wear helmets and, as Christians as well as members of the human race, be responsibile.

Smoking

Those innocent-looking but lethal ciggies.

In spite of all the health warnings more and more young people take up smoking. More and more mature people are trying to give up the habit. It, too, may eventually kill you. Have you ever seen a person die of lung cancer or liver failure? I have. And they were not really old either. Girls have an additional serious problem in that cigarette-smoking affects the baby's development in the womb, and taints the breast milk.

We also have to think of the pollution smoking causes and the effect your smoke has on others who have to breathe in the foul air you create. Asthma is on the increase even in very young children. Pollution of the atmosphere is one of the causes. Can you be said to be Christian as you wreck your own health, put others at risk and knowingly destroy the purity of the atmosphere? *Did you realise that the nicotine in cigarettes is as potent a drug as heroin?* Added to that, do your sums and you'll find that smoking costs a bomb! Couldn't you save for something really worthwhile instead? Smoking also causes bad breath so smokers aren't too pleasant to kiss.

Solvent Abuse – means sniffing substances in which chemicals are present – glues, certain paint thinners, aerosol sprays, petrol etc. These can do a lot of harm to your system. So don't think that it's daring fun.

CHAPTER 13

ARE YOU A MEANY?

Bullying – Abuse
(Discuss the role-play situations on pp. 113-119.)

Anyone who inflicts his or her will on someone else is a bully. A bully causes another person to suffer emotionally or physically. The following are some characteristic approaches of a bully (adults can be bullies too!):

- Slagging, jeering, name-calling
- Pushing a person out of the group
- Taking or breaking their belongings
- Forcing someone to do something for you
- Hitting a person; belittling someone's efforts
- Ganging up against someone
- 'Messing' in a way that hurts someone
- Spreading mean or untrue gossip about a person
- Threatening someone

This list does not describe the characteristics of an attractive or Christian person, does it? To bully someone knowingly is a sin.

The bully is often found to be a person with problems in her or his life. He or she will tend to choose quiet, shy, smaller people to bully. People who are fat, unusually tall or who have some less usual characteristic are also bullied. Others in a group may go along with the bully because they fear her or him. Few thoughtful people admire a bully.

If someone is bullying you in any of the ways listed, avoid that person when you can. If you see him or her approaching walk away. If the bully surprises you, face up to him or her and say, loudly and clearly, 'GET OUT OF MY WAY'. Then walk off smartly (don't scurry away fearfully).

Tell a parent or teacher about any persistent bullying. Most adults will be tactful, understanding and helpful. Decent classmates will have the courage to stand up for you.

Bullying is *abuse* of another person. Another form of abuse is to touch some other person on her or his private parts ('private parts' are those parts of your body that are covered by your swimsuit). These parts are very personal, genital parts having to do the responsible and important functions connected with sex and child-bearing.

Our bodies are the special places into which we welcome the living presence of God who loves through us (see pp. 12 & 15). It is obvious then that we respect and protect our unique bodies from curious and rude abuse.

> No one should open your clothes to touch or look at your private parts, nor should they try to show theirs to you.

Of course it is normal that people see one another's bodies in the ordinary course of living: boys see each other in the shower-room. Girls are often together when changing for sports or staying overnight with a pal. If you have a pain or soreness in your private parts a doctor will examine you or a parent may apply a healing cream to a sore place. I think you understand very well the difference between normal, respectful approaches and vulgar ones.

If someone (whether a young person, an adult or a relation), attempts to make vulgar or abusive approaches you must report this to an adult (parent, relation, teacher, counsellor, etc.). If the abusing person has asked you to keep it secret, it is a bad secret, so do not keep it to yourself. Tell! Don't be afraid to tell. It is not your fault that someone chooses to treat you with disrespect and vulgarity. The person may have a problem in his or her own life and need help from an adult. (For books on bullying see the book list on p. 124.)

We have been discussing various aspects of growing-up – your values, your behaviour, your thinking – and some difficulties and challenges which most young people will meet along the way.

Discuss the following

Suppose Christ were speaking in your town or village this evening. Crowds would attend. What might he say about reckless driving, drunkenness, drug-abuse, bullying, sex abuse? As followers of Christ we should know his thinking and courageously support it.

CHAPTER 14

THEN CAME BABY

Boys and Girls Become Men and Women!
Now I want to talk about male and female development and about reproducing babies.

Since you were very young you have wondered about where babies came from. Let's look for a moment at the type of questions young children ask their parents or teachers. I'll give you their typical questions and the adult's simple answers.

The answers are all true and suited to a small child. Of course not all the questions pour out one after another. They will be asked now and again over a few years. By the age of about nine most of the following questions have been asked by the young child. See what you think of the answers an adult will have given to the under nines.

Question Mum, where did Mrs Murphy get her new baby? (Go on! Try to answer that as though to a 4-year-old!)

Answer The baby grew inside her tummy. Every baby grows inside its Mum in a special place called the womb (like 'room') until it is big enough to come out into the world. A tiny baby is safe and warm and comfortable there so close to its Mum all the time.

Question How does the baby get out of the Mum?

Answer There is a very special little opening between

the Mum's legs, called the vagina, it's like a little passageway that stretches enough to let the baby come out, and the Mum and Dad are so excited to see their little son or daughter for the first time. We didn't know if you were going to be a boy baby or a girl baby so we were just longing to see you.

Question How did you know I was a girl?

Answer Well, God made boys and girls differently. A boy has a penis – you know how Sally's baby brother is? And girls have a vagina. So that's how you know whether a new baby is a boy or a girl.

Question Can Dads have babies?

Answer Only Mums have that little place inside them – the womb – in which they carry babies for about nine months. The Dad gives lots and lots of love and help to the Mum so that she can rest and be happy while she is waiting for their baby. At the very start of a baby the Dad has a very important part to play.

You see, so that the little egg (called the ovum) inside the Mum can grow into a baby, it must be joined by a tiny seed (called the sperm) from the Dad. So every baby is made by a Mum and a Dad and given life by God.

Question Where does the Dad get the seed? Does he buy it?

Answer Oh no! It is a much more special way. Do you remember I told you that the tiny egg ripens inside the Mum? Well, a little sperm ripens inside the Dad. And when his sperm meets her egg, a baby is given life.

Question How does the Dad give the Mum the seed?

Answer Do you remember we were saying that boys

and men have a penis and girls and women have a vagina? Well, the seed that is made in the Dad's body (the sperm) travels into his penis and when the Mum and Dad are hugging each other closely, there are certain very special times when he slips his penis into her vagina and leaves the sperm there. Then the sperm travels up inside the Mum and if there is a tiny egg ripe the sperm joins the egg, and that's how a baby begins. God gives it life and loves it from that very moment – as do the Mum and Dad, of course.

Question Could I get a baby in my tummy?

Answer God wants people to help him make babies, but not until they are grown up and married and have a home for the three of them. But when you are grown up, that may well be what will happen for you. Then, if you have a baby, I'll be a Granny!

So these are the early questions and answers – discuss them and add any other questions your little brother or sister may have asked.

CHAPTER 15

THE BOY'S BODY

Hormones are chemicals produced in the body's glands which control a variety of bodily processes.

In the boy's body there is a special sex hormone, testosterone, which enters the bloodstream and gradually makes a boy manly. It comes from the two glands called *testes* or *testicles* (sometimes called 'balls'). These testicles are in a loose sac called the *scrotum*, which is situated behind the *penis*. The testicles are outside the abdomen because they manufacture sperm which needs a cooler temperature in which to thrive. In cold weather (or after a swim in cold water) the scrotum gets more wrinkly as it draws the testicles closer to the body for the right level of warmth. The testicles begin to go into action at puberty. At this time *pubic hair* begins to grow in the area of the sex organs and in the arm-pits. A boy's breasts may swell a bit and feel a little sore to touch. But that will settle down when the hormones sort themselves out (You are *not* developing breasts like a girl!). All boys and men develop a ring of dark flesh around the nipple. The boy's *penis* gradually gets larger as does the scrotum behind it. Penis size varies and a smaller penis is just as effective and functions just as well as a larger one.

Around this time the boy becomes more *muscular*. *Height* and *appetite* increase. The *larynx* (voice box) develops and the 'Adams Apple' will become noticeable in a short time. That makes the voice change from the light voice of a child into the deeper voice of a man. *Sweat* increases (so you should wash or shower regularly). You'll soon sprout some hair on your face. Male sex cells called *sperm* start being produced in the testes.

During the time that these changes are taking place – and remember, this happens slowly and very gradually, not overnight! – a boy's attitude towards girls becomes a bit different. He begins to fancy girls. All this is as God planned it to be, so it is natural and good.

A great thing that begins to happen during this stage of development is the experience of an *erection and emission of semen.*

Let me explain. Down the centre of the penis there is a tube called the *urethra*. This carries *urine* (waste fluid) from the bladder. The urine comes through a little opening at the tip of the penis (called the *glans*). You've known that all your life! The glans is covered by a fold of skin called the *foreskin*.

But in adolescence, when your testes are manufacturing the minute little cells called sperm a new event takes place. The sperm are so tiny that they are invisible to the naked eye. They are carried in a whitish fluid called *semen* (or *seminal fluid*) which nourishes them. Other glands – the seminal vesicle and the prostate gland (see diagram on p. 58), contribute this nourishing liquid. One teaspoon contains millions of sperm. A mature man produces millions of sperm regularly.

The penis, which is usually limp, sometimes becomes stiff

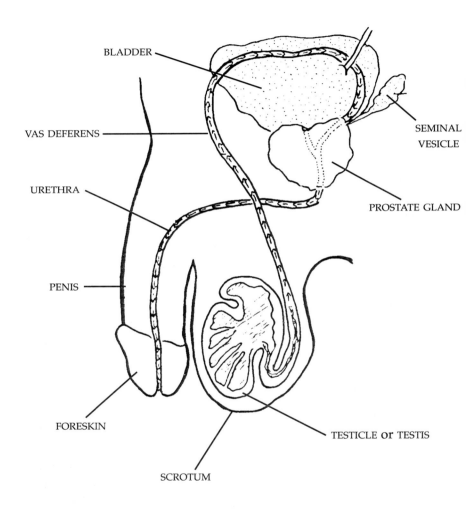

BLADDER

VAS DEFERENS

URETHRA

PENIS

FORESKIN

SCROTUM

SEMINAL VESICLE

PROSTATE GLAND

TESTICLE or TESTIS

The Male Reproductive Organs
(SIDE VIEW)

and erect. This is called an erection. Some boys call it a 'hard' or refer to themselves as being 'horny'. When the penis is erect, semen (containing sperm) can travel through it and come out of the body through the tip of the penis. So it is possible for both semen and urine to pass from the penis. But the two functions are independent. At the time when semen is passed, the bladder is closed off, so urine cannot be passed in those minutes.

Emission of Semen ('Wet Dreams')
Sometimes the boy's body manufactures an excess of seed and he may experience an erection (a 'hard') of his penis and some semen comes out of his penis. This is called an *ejaculation* (or emission of semen). Because it often happens when the boy is in bed asleep, it is called a 'wet dream'. The dream may be about something to do with sex and girls, but not always. Anyway, we don't always remember what a dream was about. The boy can sponge off the semen from the sheet or his pyjamas, or can use a tissue to mop it up. It happens to all men and boys so there is no need to feel embarrassed about it. It shows that your body is beginning to function in a manly way. The feeling of the erection and the semen coming out is pleasant.

Sometimes the penis becomes erect for other reasons. You will have noticed it happening occasionally when you were a little boy. But little boys do not produce sperm and semen. An erection can come as result of tension, nervousness or excitement – or the need to go to the toilet. Erections can occur during the day too when you are up and about. It can happen when looking at a sexy film or video or when you see a girl you fancy.

The erection can subside if you distract yourself from it and concentrate on other doings or activities that really interest

you. There is no more need to be anxious about these natural happenings than you would be anxious about a sneeze.

It is advisable for lads to wear trousers that are not too tight as the sex organs are most healthy in cool conditions without the pressure of clothing such as tight jeans.

Masturbation means handling the sexual (genital) organs to try to produce erection and ejaculation. These are pleasurable feelings. So masturbation is a natural and understandable impulse. But because it can distort the natural purpose of sex and encourage a quick release of tension, it needs some discipline and control. If a man develops a habit of masturbation it may be difficult for him to give his wife the time for the gradual love-making that gives her such pleasure. Human sexual powers were designed to be shared in loving intimacy. Masturbation, if uncontrolled, can cause a person to be overly self-centred even when with their marriage partner.

Women are also tempted to touch their private parts in order to excite themselves sexually. Both boys and girls can learn to discipline the impulse.

If a person is masturbating excessively it can well be an indication that there is a deeper life problem which they need to discuss with an understanding adult – parent, teacher, doctor or counsellor. Sometimes there is vulgar talk about masturbation. But you leave that behind as you become more mature.

CHAPTER 16

NASTIES

Pornography (Films, videos, books, magazines, etc. in which there is horrifying violence and/or when sex is distorted and vulgarised).

Pornography is often called 'porn' and it is advisable to avoid it. It is sexually arousing in a crude and vulgar way. If you choose to use 'blue' or X-rated movies or porn films or magazines to entertain and excite yourself you are poisoning your system. It takes a long time to get rid of the sour taste and superficial thrills of vulgar, lustful talk and behaviour before you can share the joy of God-given beautiful, sensitive human love. A diet of bad language, dirty stories and degrading pictures of nudes brutalises beauty and separates it from love. It is *love* that we all need, not brutality.

Avoid comics and films or videos which degrade people – especially women. People who produce pornography are cruelly making money from the curiosity and vulnerability of other people. Refuse to be drawn into their squalid and dehumanising world. Refuse to debase what God made so beautiful. Don't curse and do not use the sacred name of Jesus as a swear word (a bad habit in Ireland).

Be your own censor.
Keep out the filth.

Girls, too, can be vulgar, foul-mouthed and cheap. They sometime encourage such obscenity and crudeness in boys by laughing and being afraid to object. Have the courage to show that such talk is a turn-off for you. Walk away if it continues.

Be Happily Occupied
God designed our sexual natures and he wants us to find happiness in being girls/boys, men/women.

It is a good thing to be happily occupied. 'Couch potatoes' slouched in a chair watching any old TV programme are missing opportunities for developing their personalities and becoming interesting people. Sports, reading and other hobbies can be great sources of fun and interest. Chasing, running, kicking ball, climbing, cycling, swimming or rounders are great for the system and encourage healthy development.

Boys and girls often play together and make good pals. I hope you can visit one another's homes and have fun, chat and play games together. Don't expect your parents to lay on food and entertainment for you and your friends. A 'cuppa' and a biscuit is fine. And don't complain of *boredom*. Other people shouldn't have to think up your activities. Dig deep into your personality and discover how you can get into enjoyable pastimes. Be a bit original and creative. The cry 'Mum, I'm bored' is pathetic. You are old enough to think out things to do and make, and discover

people to share with. Dig the garden, take the dog (or the baby) for a walk, clean out your bedroom, do some housework to surprise your Mum, bake a cake or chop some wood – anything. But don't complain of boredom.

By chatting in groups you will get to know and be able to relax with lads and girls who live nearby.

> Make a list of all the things you could do when next you feel at a loose end – things you would enjoy doing for yourself and be glad to do for others.

CHAPTER 17

THE GIRL'S BODY

Girls begin to experience puberty (bodily changes) any time from about ten to sixteen years of age. It doesn't matter whether your development is early on or later. It is quite normal that the starting bell rings at different stages for different people. It is important not to jeer, tease or bully people because of the stage of bodily development they have reached. We're all different. Variation in rate and time of development is quite normal with young people all over the world.

At puberty a girl, too, develops hair under her arms and pubic hair which is a little triangle of hair in the area of her vagina. She also tends to perspire more at this time and should shower or wash well every day to keep herself fresh.

While a boy will be flat-chested, a girl begins to grow breasts. (Don't mind if one seems to be a little bigger than the other during development. That quite often happens. You will not end up with one big breast and one small one!)

Breasts can be a little sore and tender as they develop – nothing much and quite normal. You will notice a ring of dark, pinkish flesh surrounding the nipple and you may feel a slight thickening behind the nipple where the milk ducts are situated. (They don't go into action until a woman has a baby.)

Breast-feeding: The purpose of breasts is to produce milk with which to feed a baby. Breast-feeding is a happy and relaxing experience for a mother. Her breasts produce just the right milk for her baby at just the right temperature. And the baby loves it. It is lovely to hold your baby so close and feel it cuddling in to you as it sucks busily. Only a few minutes sucking is enough for a 'meal'. Then there is the burping, the nappy change, the little chat and a hug before settling the baby down to sleep again.

Usually after a few months the Mum introduces the baby to bottle feeding and tiny mouthfuls of food off a spoon.

Some mothers may choose or be advised by their doctor to put the baby on bottle feeds immediately after the birth. If the baby isn't sucking at the nipples, the breast won't continue to produce milk. The milk will go away and there will be no further milk in the mother's breasts until her next baby is born. So the only women with milk in their breasts are those who have a new baby which they are breast-feeding.

Breasts come in different sizes – just like the other parts of our bodies. There is no 'ideal' size. Milk will come to small breasts as well as to the bigger ones. And small-breasted women are attractive to men just as women with larger breasts are.

Bras: Measure your breasts with an inch-tape. First, measure your chest size by bringing the inch-tape around your rib cage just under your breasts. Add five inches to the measurement. This will give you your bra size. Measure around the biggest part of your breasts to get your cup size. If the measurement is the same as your bra size, your cup size is A. If it is one inch more, your cup size is B, and so on. All good department stores offer a confidential fitting and advisory service, so don't feel embarrassed to ask for help.

It is not essential that you wear a bra. The choice is yours. It is just a matter of being comfortable. Often a BV (bra-vest) or 'crop-top' is chosen at your age. Later, as the breasts become bigger and, for example, a girl feels her breasts are a bit floppy when she runs, a bra enhances her figure. Lots of young teenagers prefer not to wear a bra during early development. Breasts really are a wonderful part of God's design; they look nice and have such an important job to do.

Other changes: At this time a girl's hips broaden a little and her waist becomes slim. Naturally she likes to look good. But do remember, a bright, warm-hearted and caring personality is much more important than physical good looks. So don't forget to smile and keep your teeth and hair clean and shining.

But! A Word of Warning
Watch the sweets! And cut down on chocolate, crisps, fat, fries, pastries and snacks between meals.

Just don't allow weight to creep up. Good balanced meals with plenty of salads, fruit and veg are best for all of us.

Take plenty of exercise, both outdoor and indoor; swimming, running, gymnastics, walking, cycling and dancing are all great for you.

CHAPTER 18

WHAT GOES ON INSIDE?

A girl's main sexual organs are *inside* her body. Because a woman carries a baby inside her for nine months before its birth, the baby must be safe, comfortable and well-protected. The womb (or uterus) is a perfectly designed place for the tiny unborn baby. It is one of the main sex organs which include the *fallopian tubes,* the *ovaries* and the *vagina* (see diagram on p. 72).

Down between your legs you have three openings. Two of them are for going to the toilet to pass waste fluid (urine) and waste food (faeces).

But the third opening is right in the centre between the other two. It is a small opening which, in a young girl, is covered over with a layer of skin called the *hymen.* The opening leads to the *vagina* which is a passageway leading to the *womb.* The vagina is quite slim but made of material which can stretch sufficiently to let a baby come out of its mother's womb. The hymen of a young girl will open gradually sometimes as a result of gymnastics, horse-riding or other sporting activities. It is normal that it should eventually be broken as the girl becomes a woman.

So *the vagina is the passageway leading to the womb* (see diagram on p. 72). The womb is pear-shaped and about the size of the palm of your hand. It is capable of stretching and expanding to accommodate a baby growing inside it.

If you look at the diagram (p. 72) you will see that there are two *fallopian tubes,* one on either side of the top of the womb and there are two grape-sized *ovaries* connected by fibres to the outside of the womb. From the time of her birth a girl has thousands of *ova* (eggs) stored in her ovaries. Each little *ovum* (egg) is about the size of a full-stop on this page.

At puberty the ova begin to mature and each month (or about every 25-28 days) an ovum ripens fully and is released from the ovary. (If a woman is going to have twins or triplets – two or three eggs are released simultaneously (p. 93). The ripening of the ovum is called *ovulation*. The ovaries also produce hormones – *oestrogen* and *progesterone*. The oestrogen travels through the bloodstream to make the girl's body womanly. Progesterone is the chemical which prepares the womb for a baby to live in.

The ripe ovum is received into the fallopian tube and begins its journey to the womb. It is during the days when the ovum is travelling through the fallopian tube that the woman will become pregnant if she has sexual intercourse (explained later). These days are her *fertile days*. On other days in the month she will not become pregnant because there will not be an ovum making its journey to the womb. She would be *infertile* (or else she might be already pregnant. During the nine months of pregnancy no new eggs come from the ovaries.). If the ovum (egg) is not joined by a male sperm it continues its lone journey to the womb and passes out of the vagina unnoticed.

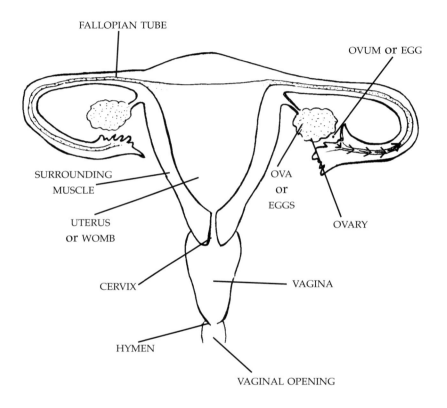

NAVEL

FALLOPIAN TUBE

OVUM or EGG

SURROUNDING
MUSCLE

OVA
or
EGGS

UTERUS
or WOMB

OVARY

CERVIX

VAGINA

HYMEN

VAGINAL OPENING

The Female Reproductive Organs

CHAPTER 19

FROM GIRL TO WOMAN

Menstruation (period)

While the ovum is travelling down the fallopian tube towards the womb, the womb is busy preparing a soft lining of blood and tissue to make a little nest. If, on its journey, the ovum has met a male sperm and a baby is conceived, the womb will be ready for the baby to nestle in for its nine months (40 weeks) of development.

But when a baby is not conceived, the ovum reaches the womb, dies away and then the blood and tissue which had lined the womb are not going to be needed for a baby. So the blood and tissue become thin and trickle gently down through the vagina. This is called a *period* (or menstruation).

This usually happens to a woman every 26-30 days, lasts for 4-5 days and then stops. The next month the process is repeated. So a mature woman has a period each month (or so) which lasts for about 5 days.

In adolescent girls periods may start any time between 10 and 16 years of age. At first, while the body is getting used to its new function, periods can be irregular and last for two to perhaps, seven days. Don't worry if you have periods at irregular intervals. Gradually, as you grow more mature, the periods should settle down. (An adult woman has no periods during the nine months of pregnancy.)

When the girl sees the first little spots of blood (brownish or red) she places a sanitary towel inside her knickers. The towel is made of soft material like cotton wool, backed with a fine plastic and encased in a tissue-like envelope. It is like a little nappy. It absorbs the trickle of blood. Sanitary towels are changed every few hours during the days of the period. You wear one at night too to protect your nightie or pyjamas from being stained.

A celebration
Tell your Mum when this happens. Remember that she has been expecting it to happen and will be delighted. Your Dad, too, knows about girls of your age starting periods. So perhaps you'd have a bit of a celebration.

Many mothers keep packets of sanitary towels (or pantie-pads) at home. Its a good idea to have a packet in your own room even if you have not yet started your periods. If your breasts have started to develop, period time is not too many months away.

There are different makes and thickness of towel but basically they are all made of the same sort of material and are soft and comfortable to wear.

If your periods start in school, you can tell the teacher. There is always a supply of STs (sanitary towels) in girls' schools so that girls can get them easily. Sometimes they are available from slot machines in the cloakroom or washroom. It is a good idea, once you reach puberty, to keep an ST (or pantie-pad) in an envelope in the bottom of your schoolbag. It can make you feel secure if your period takes you unawares.

Normal and healthy
Periods are a normal and healthy occurrence, not sore like the bleeding of a wound. The bleeding doesn't gush out. It comes gently, stops and starts a bit and lasts for three to six days each month. After a few hours, when the ST has

absorbed quite a bit of the flow it is time to change to a fresh one. There is not a fixed number to use. It is according to your comfort. Only about two tablespoons of blood are lost during the whole 4/5 days of an average period. So that's not much.

Some sanitary towels cannot be flushed down the toilet. Read the instructions on the packet. A used towel can be wrapped in toilet-tissue (or placed in a little bag provided in women's toilets) and placed in a bin or incinerator which is usually beside the toilet. At home your Mum will tell you how best to dispose of used towels. Usually they can be well wrapped in a plastic bag and put in the bin.

Your uterus (womb) contracts – like tightening up – to send the period down and the contractions can cause a cramp or tummy-ache at the start of a period. You may need to take a painkiller such as you would use for a headache. If you are a bit crampy, lie on your bed when you come in from school and place a warm hot-water bottle on your tummy. Relax with a nice warm drink.

Remember

All girls get monthly periods, even sports stars, pop stars, musicians, artists and models. And they all cope very well. So you, too, will get very used to the natural monthly period days.

Tampons are an *internal* form of sanitary wear.

A tampon is a cigar-shaped cylinder of absorbent material which is inserted into the vagina where it absorbs the flow of blood. It has a little cord attached which remains outside the vagina. To remove the tampon after a few hours, simply pull the cord gently – out comes the used tampon and it can be flushed down the toilet. The tampon cannot travel beyond the cervix and fits comfortably into the vagina. The removal cord rarely breaks. Should it break, it is still quite simple to remove the tampon. It is important to remember to remove the final tampon on the last day of your period. The manufacturers of tampons give a warning that a rare disease called Toxic Shock Syndrome (TSS) can occur very occasionally in women using tampons. So if you get a sudden high fever or rash, remove the tampon immediately and consult your doctor.

Tampons can be difficult for a young girl to use; the entrance to the vagina may not yet be sufficiently open to enable insertion of the tampon. I advise young girls to start by using STs rather than tampons. Your Mum will chat about all this with you.

Vaginal discharge
Even before a girl's periods begin she may from time to time notice a whitish or yellowish stain on her knickers. This is a normal vaginal discharge. Its purpose is to cleanse and lubricate the vagina in a healthy way. Periods may not occur for quite a few months after you first notice the discharge. Just remember to keep yourself clean and wash out your panties regularly. A pantie-liner (like a very slim ST) can be used if the discharge is a little more at times. Just make yourself comfortable.

If you have a soreness or an itch or a burning sensation in your vaginal area it may be an infection. Tell your mother and she can go with you to the doctor. It's no big deal, so don't worry!

Some people feel a bit tired, tense or moody at period time or just before their period starts. Try to rest and make things pleasant for yourself (and, incidentally, for others). Remember to cut down on your intake of salt and don't take ice-cold food or drinks. A warm bath is a comfort. If your mother, friend or sister is a bit cranky around their period time be understanding and cheer them up with a bit of praise, help and a nice 'cuppa' for a surprise. That will do you good too.

Sometimes girls say that 'boys are lucky because they don't have periods'. But periods become a normal part of life; you get so used to them. Boys have to work hard and discipline their sexual urges. In this context girls must be careful to wear modest clothes and not invite boys to behave badly with them.

Boys, too, should be understanding of the monthly physical and emotional experiences of girls and women. Be aware, for example, that if a girl refuses to go for a swim it may be because she has a period. So don't insist further. (Tampons are very useful for girls who swim at period time).

Menopause (or 'change of life')
In her late 40s or by about 50 years of age a woman's periods stop. They gradually come to an end, after which the woman will not become pregnant again. She can still enjoy sex with her husband but she will not conceive another baby.

CHAPTER 20

GETTING TOGETHER

Sexual Intercourse
Having looked at the amazing way in which the male and female sex organs work, how sperm and ova are produced (and I have just described it all in outline), let's discuss how sexual intercourse takes place.

> **Sexual Intercourse** is for mature people who have made a commitment to one another to live together 'for better or for worse, in sickness and in health' until the end of life. That is a promise for adults only and it reflects God's promise to us: 'I shall never leave you'.

Sexual intercourse is sometimes called 'having sex'. When a husband and wife make love they kiss and cuddle one another, tell each other of their love and hold one another closely and tenderly.

When they are so close they both feel excited and joyful. The man's penis becomes erect and he knows that the semen (and sperm) have come into it. The woman's vagina feels damp because glands in the vagina produce a lubricating fluid to moisten the vagina and make it easy for the man's erect penis to slip in.

The man slips his penis into his wife's vagina, moving it in and out for a few minutes until the semen comes out and enters the woman. They both feel excited and make sounds of pleasure. Then, having delivered his semen, the man withdraws his penis and the intercourse is over. They continue to embrace and hold one another until they relax. Sexual intercourse is enjoyable for both partners and, of course, it doesn't hurt. (No-one would want do it if it hurt, and then we'd have no babies!)

The single exception to this is that if the woman's hymen (see p. 70) is not fully broken there may be a moment of a little soreness on the first act of sexual intercourse. Then she knows that will not occur again. So she is happy about it. A good husband is very gentle at the first act of intercourse particularly, so that his wife will not mind the pinch of soreness she may experience.

We also know of people who have sexual intercourse before they are married (see p. 87). We must never judge anyone else. Only God knows and understands the situation of each individual. However, the Bible teaches that the ideal to aim at is to keep sexual intercourse for the committed relationship of marriage where the two people promise themselves to one another, before witnesses and before God. Through the priest or minister, God blesses them and promises to be with them always.

CHAPTER 21

STARTING OUT

How it starts – 'Going with' someone or dating
It is natural that boys and girls meet in groups, play together and get to know one another. Some go to youth clubs or swimming or take part in other sports together.

Around about the age of 12 girls and boys may begin to look at one another in a different way. You may feel attracted to a particular person of the opposite sex – fancy him or her. That's a normal feeling. Or you may just like to be pals. (See John and Anne's story on pp. 113-119.)

Other lads or girls may not fancy anyone yet: it doesn't happen to everyone at exactly the same time! Sometimes the boys living around are rough and rude and not particularly nice or good fun to be with. That may be because shyness causes them to put on a show-off or macho image which is not attractive to all girls. There will always be nice fellows but sometimes the showing-off (smoking, using foul language, horseplay) gives a bad impression. A few girls may join in but other girls – more shy and gentle – prefer to be with their girlfriends. Boys too, can be shy and prefer to be with their mates rather than facing the 'going-with-a-girl' business too soon.

We are all unique and free to develop at our own pace. Just because a few lads or girls in your class fancy a person of the opposite sex doesn't mean that everyone has to. The really attractive boy or girl may not have turned up yet, or the particular *chemicals which cause attraction between male and female* may not have become active – in many adolescents this doesn't happen until they are into their teens.

You may not meet a person you fancy living locally. Perhaps your special person will turn up when you are on holidays or visiting relations in the country or on the other side of town. So be content to wait and enjoy your free time doing just what makes you feel happy. There is no hurry into the next phase of life.

> Don't let anyone put pressure on you to 'go with' or 'get off with' a person of the opposite sex. Just say 'I'm choosy and haven't met the right one yet'. Say it with a smile!

It's always a bit scary to move from the peaceful waters of childhood into the choppy sea of adolescence. Nature guides you gently so go slowly with whatever pace feels good to you.

Those who talk and laugh a lot about sex and 'going-with' people are not necessarily more grown-up than, or superior to those who decide not to get into that business yet. Both types are okay people who must be responsible for the consequences of their choices.

Discuss: What might be the consequences of 'going with' someone at your age?

CHAPTER 22

DON'T RUSH IN

Dating is about making friends
Some adolescents tend to think that when you find a particularly attractive person of the opposite sex the first step is to ask that person to 'go with you' (become your 'one and only' for a while). That means cutting yourselves off from other attractive lads/girls who may come on the scene. Sometimes it's like trying to 'own' the other person and that never works.

Added to that, it is thought that if someone agrees to 'go with you' or 'meet' you, you have to then 'get off' with one another! ('Get off' means 'French' or open-mouthed kissing.) That can be quite a threat to many boys and girls.

It is natural not to want to close-kiss a person you barely know. Close kissing is for people who, over a long time, have made a deep, dependable friendship. (See qualities of friendship and love on p. 16). No-one makes a deep friendship quickly. So, 'getting off', if it means French kissing, is inappropriate for adolescents. Often it has nothing to do with love and is only for experimentation or maybe because you think that the other person expects it! Sometimes people think that *love* is the same thing as *lust* (which is just strong sexual desire). The trouble about sexual touching and French kissing is that they are part of nature's plan for leading people to an intense desire for full sexual intercourse. When it would be wrong (sinful) to have sexual intercourse, young people must content themselves with a light kiss and a hug. It is not at all easy to call a halt to intense 'snogging', 'petting' and 'necking'. Each person, when sexually excited, desires more and more closeness. So keep it brief and light.

Some people boast about 'getting off'. Since it takes no intelligence to kiss intimately, it is not a thing to boast about. Anyone could do it. People of strong character control the desire for such closeness until the appropriate time when real friendship and caring have developed between them.

Adolescents can feel love and sexual attraction. It is quite normal that some will have these feelings. But remember, true love protects and does what is best, in the long term, for the loved one. You have every right to say 'No' to behaviour which you feel is not the best thing for either of you at your age. (Don't forget 'Assertiveness' p. 40.)

> Sexual intercourse is against civil law for people under 16 years of age.

If you want to be special friends with someone, you can smilingly and in a straightforward way suggest a date. If the other person turns down the suggestion don't be hurt. He or she may not feel ready yet, may not be allowed by those at home, or may feel that you don't know each other well enough.

> **D.I.Y.**
> If you want to 'go with' a certain person don't ask a pal to ask the other person on your behalf. *Do it yourself!*

If you do start being special friends spell out the terms.

What might the terms be? Discuss.

Friendships do break up
If you have been going out together for quite a while either one of you may find that you are not getting on as well as you had hoped. You may, like many teenagers, tire of the way in which the 'twosome-ness' is cutting you off from meeting new friends. Explain to your friend that, though you would like to continue to be friends, you feel that you no longer want to be tied-down to 'going together'. Even though the other person may be disappointed and hurt there is no sense in continuing to pretend that you still feel as you originally did. Be honest and kind in making the break. Both of you will be the better for mixing with groups of boys and girls and gaining experience of other characters and other approaches to life. Such breaks are painful and you may be a bit more careful about saying 'Yes' too quickly next time. That's the way we learn about real life. Maturity will be creeping in all the time.

CHAPTER 23

WHY WAIT?

Pregnant but unmarried

Looking at films, videos and magazines would make you think that every fellow and girl who are going out together very soon have sexual intercourse. Dr Gerard Sheehan of the American Centre for Disease Control recently advised that for their first experience of sexual intercourse people should be in their twenties and in a mutually faithful relationship. For practising Christians this is the time for marriage.

Films, videos and romantic stories don't often tell the real-life results. As I told you, lovemaking is beautiful, exciting and good between married people. But if lads and girls try lovemaking on dates they can lose control of the situation. Sexual intercourse may take place and the girl may become pregnant.

No joy!

When she misses her next period the girl may be deeply shocked and wonder 'could I be pregnant?' 'Did he really love me or did he just use me?'. The boy is frightened by her questions. Maybe he tries to reassure her. Or perhaps they both realise that they have not valued or taken responsibility for one another. Perhaps they are now the parents of a unique child who will need a mother, a father and a loving home. They may have used a condom (see pp. 98 & 103) but a considerable percentage of condoms fail – especially when used by teenagers. Perhaps neither has a job; maybe they are studying still and have no money.

Often the boy goes off, refusing to take any responsibility for his own baby and its mother. They may both realise that if only they had loved enough they would have talked more seriously about the consequences – physical and emotional

– of having sexual intercourse before the time was right to express their love that way. The girl is faced with a nine month pregnancy. Girls often show great courage in facing this responsibility alone. We should do all we can to comfort and help such a girl. She may choose to have her baby adopted or she may decide to keep it. From that day her life has changed. She must play the part of two parents which may mean giving up her job or study, her independence and much of her social life. Some boyfriends are courageous and co-operative. Boys and girls must think very deeply about the anguish that this situation can cause one another, their child and the families involved. Real love seeks to protect the loved person from such heartbreak.

In the USA, in spite of available contraception (see p. 98) one million teenagers become pregnant each year. Three million contract sexually transmitted diseases (STD – see p. 101).

In the last few years groups of young Americans have come together and decided to sign covenant cards (promises), promising to remain pure and not have sexual intercourse until marriage. One group I heard of is called 'Make Love Last' (a good double meaning). In another group they each wear a special ring indicating that they are keeping sex for marriage.

Another 'rave' community, 'Straight Edge', have committed themselves to no sex, no alcohol, no drugs.

Couldn't some of our adolescents set up similar groups?

CHAPTER 24

NEW LIFE

How conception of a baby takes place
Remember when I described sexual intercourse between husband and wife (p. 79). Do you think that the wife would always become pregnant after having sex? A lot of young people think that.

However, even though the husband passes the semen-covered sperm into his wife's vagina, she will not always become pregnant.

The thousands of minute sperm race up to see if there is a ripe ovum (egg) in the fallopian tubes. But there is only a ripe egg there at certain times of the month. So unless they had sexual intercourse in the fertile time (the time that an egg was travelling down the fallopian tube) pregnancy would not occur. The sperm would wait around a little while hoping that the next ripe egg would pop out. But if it isn't ready to do so the sperm just dies off. So, you see, pregnancy can only occur if sex takes place during the woman's fertile time. For many days of each month (menstrual cycle) there will be no egg ready. The husband and wife enjoy intercourse, sharing their love in this special way, whether or not a baby results. A woman can be taught to identify her fertile days.

This time – a baby!
At the fertile time of the month a ripe egg is present in the fallopian tube (either the left or the right tube, depending on which ovary it has come from). When the couple have sex, the sperm race up (some delicate ones die on the way) only about 100 sperm reach the tube. The sperm group

around the egg (ovum) and just one sperm is the lucky one. It penetrates the egg and a new life begins. This tiny new life continues to travel to the womb (uterus) which (as described on p. 73) is already beautifully prepared to receive it. The new little being (called an *embryo* at this stage) roots itself to its mother and a cord reaches from the mother to the embryo. The *placenta* is the sponge-like organ in the mother's womb from which the *umbilical cord* carries food and oxygen into the baby through its belly-button. The cord transfers the waste food back to the mother's system which disposes of it quiet automatically.

The *umbilical cord* is a lifeline. It brings *oxygen* and *food* to the baby in the womb and also *removes waste products* from the baby's system.

That is how the baby is nourished for its nine months in the womb.

A husband and wife may have sexual intercourse during pregnancy unless the doctor advises against it. The *cervix* (the doorway to the womb) is closed so that the sperm simply enters the vagina and comes right out again. The woman does not produce any further ripe ova (eggs) during the nine months of pregnancy. Neither does she have a period because the blood and tissue are retained in the womb for the developing baby.

From the moment when the ovum and sperm join to form one cell (the baby or embryo), a new, unique and precious human being exists. Nothing extra is added. God has so designed it that the male and female cells have instructions – called *genes* – built into them. These genes give information about how this special baby will develop – maybe it will have brown eyes like its Dad, curly hair like its Mum, be good at sport like Dad and artistic like Mum – and even have some resemblance to a Grandad or some talent inherited from another family member. Isn't that amazing? A child's development is affected by his or her surroundings, climate, food, etc.

Abortion

Imagine, then, that some people who do not want to give birth to their baby have it removed from the womb in the early months of pregnancy when it is so tiny that it dies. That operation is called abortion. The Church teaches that only God has a right to give life and take it away. Human life is sacred.

Abortion is often resorted to when contraception fails, so millions of babies who are unwanted are discarded before they have the opportunity of their right to a full life.

The first weeks of life *(in the womb)*
By 6th class both boys and girls are ready to know about the development of the baby in the womb:

DAY 1   Conception – sperm and ovum meet in fertilisation. Genetic make-up complete. Colour of eyes, hair, sex and even build determined. A unique individual is present in the womb.

DAY 17   Development of own blood cells. Placenta established.

DAY 20   Foundation of entire nervous system established.

DAY 21   Heart starts to beat. This is at least as dramatic as birth.

DAY 30   Regular blood flow within closed vascular system. Ear and nose start to develop.

DAY 42   Skeleton complete and reflexes present. Liver, kidneys and lungs formed.

DAY 43   Electrical brain-wave patterns can be recorded.

DAY 56   All organs functioning; growth and maturity are all that occur from now on, in the same way that a child grows into an adult.

DAY 65   The baby can make a fist and will grasp an object stroking his or her palm; the baby will also leap up and down in the womb with movements co-ordinated.

WEEK 16   Baby is half its birth length and its heart pumps 50 pints of blood daily.

WEEK 20   Hair appears on the head. Weight – about 1lb. Height – 12 inches.

WEEK 28   Eyes open. Baby can hear mother's digestive processes and heartbeat.

WEEK 36/40 Birth – The joy that a child has come into the world. A unique, new human being. Average weight is about 7lbs, but can vary without affecting health.

Twins

Non-identical twins are produced when, at one particular fertile time a woman produces two eggs. These are then fertilised by two separate sperm. Each twin has its own placenta. These twins may be of the same sex or one of each sex. Each is within its own bag of amniotic fluid.

Identical twins are conceived when one egg, fertilised by one sperm, almost immediately breaks into two separate individuals. They share one placenta, are always of the one sex and look exactly like each other. They share one bag of fluid but are separated within it by a thin 'wall' of cells.
Twins are usually diagnosed by the doctor at about the sixth month of pregnancy but can also be seen by means of a scan (a form of X-ray) at an earlier stage.

Siamese twins occur if the egg starts to divide but doesn't fully split. This is extremely rare. The babies are born joined at a particular part of their bodies. Later the doctor may operate to try to separate them.

Triplets (or more) babies occur when 3 (or more) eggs are produced at the same ovulation and fertilised by three (or more) sperm. Triplets can be identical or non-identical.

CHAPTER 25

THE NEW ARRIVAL

A child is born
None of us can remember what it was like to be cosy and nurtured in our mother's womb and then, one day, to receive the signal that we had to leave that comfort and be born into the world.

In the womb the baby is surrounded by warm liquid which is called amniotic fluid and can hear the mother's heartbeat and her voice.

Then, on the given day, the muscles of the uterus (womb) begin to contract pushing the baby down, usually head first, towards the cervix which expands. The baby is pressed down the widening vagina and out into the world. I wonder why we do not remember such an amazing experience.

Labour
When the mother's womb is contracting she experiences cramps which come at regular intervals. She is said to be in *labour*. Even though the cramps are painful, they are not an illness, they are natural and the mother is really excited about being able to see her baby. The amniotic fluid helps to swoosh the baby down the birth canal (vagina). Imagine how the vagina is able to stretch to let the baby through. The father is often with his wife as she gives birth. He encourages her and soothes her. He, too, is excited by this great event. Will it be a boy or a girl? The mother can have an injection of a painkiller called an epidural which numbs the area. Other mothers choose to use a mask from time to time through which they breathe pain-relieving gas and

air. So it is always possible to get relief if the cramps get really strong.

Many mothers prefer not to take any pain relief so that they are alert and fully aware of all that is happening during the birth process. A mother will have had classes and discussions in the months before the birth to help her to cope as well as possible with the great event.

Until you have had a baby you will not be able to guess how thrilling it is. Even though there is the pain of labour and the exhaustion you can rest well afterwards cuddling your baby, with both of you being cuddled by the proud new Dad.

> When you see a birth on TV it is often dramatised and can look awful! I would rather actually have a baby then look at an actress pretending to be having one. So don't let TV versions scare you.

Cutting the Cord

When the baby is born the umbilical cord is still coming from its belly-button. It is attached to the mum's placenta, which comes away at birth. (A special new placenta develops with each new baby.) The nurse cuts the cord almost as soon as the baby comes from the womb. The cutting of the cord doesn't hurt the baby. (The cord has no nerves in it so it is no more painful than cutting your nails or hair.) The cord is clamped, cut, and then has a little bandage applied while it heals. All that remains of your umbilical cord today is the little bit that may protrude from your belly-button. Your belly-button has no function after you are born.

Rest and relaxation are needed for the mother after the nine months of pregnancy and the energetic labour of giving birth. Nowadays, fathers give great help and thoroughly enjoy their baby as it gets to know them. Modern men share all the housekeeping jobs and can be very expert at them.

Getting trim again
After a few weeks the mother's body is returning to its pre-pregnancy shape and form. It takes a few months before she is fully back to normal. Breast-feeding (see p. 67) helps a lot in restoring the mother's figure. Keep-fit exercises help her to get back into shape again.

A mother doesn't usually return to the normal pattern of ovulation and periods until her baby is about six weeks old. Breast-feeding may delay ovulation even a little longer but doesn't always do so.

Miscarriage
If a baby is born before the mum is 6 to 7 months pregnant it is unlikely to survive. A baby which is born in the early months of pregnancy would be inadequately developed and couldn't live outside its mother's womb. A baby born

at such a stage is said to have been miscarried. No one is certain why miscarriages occur but they happen quite often in the first three months of pregnancy. Some experts think that miscarriages happen if the embryo is not developing normally. No one can help having a miscarriage. It is just a sad spontaneous happening of nature. A mother will usually be able to begin another healthy pregnancy after she has taken a rest of some months.

Handicap

Every healthy baby receives 23 *chromosomes* from its mother's egg ovum and 23 chromosomes from its father's sperm. That makes a total of 46 chromosomes.

If the number of chromosomes is wrongly balanced the baby will have some level of handicap. Each chromosome is made up of thousands of genes. The more we learn about all this the more we are struck with awe and wonder at God's creative genius.

There are other reasons for handicap in a baby, such as the pregnant mother contracting German measles, or the umbilical cord getting twisted and cutting off oxygen for even a brief time.

A baby with a handicap draws courage, tenderness and love from people. Perhaps that is the great gift of people with handicaps: they make us appreciate our own giftedness and, while we care for them, they so often teach us patience, trust, courage and gratitude.

Do you know anyone with a handicap?
Discuss.

CHAPTER 26

FAMILY PLANNING

Contraception means the prevention of pregnancy. The four main family planning methods you hear about are the *condom, 'The Pill', the diaphragm* and *natural methods.*

The **condom** is a sheath of thin rubber which a man draws over his penis just before sexual intercourse to prevent sperm from entering the woman.

- Condoms are not guaranteed. Sometimes they contain inherent flaws. At other times people use them carelessly without following the instructions carefully. So pregnancy can occur.

'The Pill' is a term that covers a wide variety of tablets containing hormones which prevent the normal process of ovulation (producing an ovum) in the woman. If ovulation is stopped she cannot become pregnant, although occasionally

- 'breakthrough' pregnancy occurs.
- A number of unpleasant side-effects, some serious, can occur as result of taking the Pill. It cannot be purchased without prescription.

The diaphragm (or 'cap') is a flexible rubber device used with spermicide which a woman inserts into her vagina before sex. This diaphragm must be left in the vagina for at least six hours after intercourse.

- Spermicide is a cream which should be used with condoms and diaphragms. It is for killing any sperm that may escape from the contraceptive.

- Some people are sensitive to spermicide. Care must be taken. The fitting of the diaphragm must be checked regularly as pregnancy can occur if the device is not accurately placed and well-fitting.

Natural methods of family planning involve a woman learning to keep an accurate record of her fertile time. Then the couple agree to abstain from intercourse at fertile times if they do not want another baby that year. The method is called 'natural' because no device, creams or pills are used. A new electronic way of identifying ovulation is due on the market soon. This should help women to have greater accuracy in discovering their fertile and infertile times.

- However, careless charting, irregularity or change in the menstrual cycle can result in an unplanned pregnancy.

No artificial contraceptive method is completely effective and without side-effects.

All the time new and more natural and healthy methods of family planning are being designed and tested in laboratories. So the picture changes regularly.

As you grow older you will learn more about all this.

> **Before Marriage**
> You do not have to worry about any kind
> of family planning or contraception now,
> once you have decided to keep sexual
> intercourse until marriage. (Remember
> pp. 23-24.)

Married People make the most responsible and caring
decisions they can about planning their families. Often
they consult their doctor or priest. It is a very personal and
intimate decision for each wife and husband.

Priests are encouraged to 'have a compassionate pastoral
understanding of the very real difficulties facing many
married people' (*Love is for Life*, Irish Bishop's Pastoral
Letter, 1985).

CHAPTER 27

SEXUALLY TRANSMITTED DISEASES AND AIDS

Sexually Transmitted Diseases (STDs) are often called VD (Venereal Disease). They are infections that can be transmitted from one person to another during sexual intercourse. They are usually contracted by people who have sex with a variety of partners or with someone already infected. Some STDs are developed only by men, others only by women.

The signs include soreness or itching of the private parts or pain on passing urine. (It is important to remember that simple infections can also cause soreness of the private parts and pain on passing urine. A person is well aware if they have had casual sexual intimacy which may be the cause. Those who have not done so should go to the doctor for the simple cures available.) You can see why sexual intercourse is, for many reasons, best shared with a faithful partner.

Almost every STD is curable after suitable, sometimes long-term treatment. An exception to that is the infection we know as AIDS.

AIDS (Acquired Immune Deficiency Syndrome)
AIDS is caused by a virus called HIV (Human Immuno-deficiency Virus). No one knows where it originated. As a result of the virus a person's immune system (which normally defends the body against diseases) fails to do its job. So the person gets a wide variety of illnesses which they can no longer fight off. As the person becomes increasingly ill, full-blown AIDS develops. Death follows.

The virus is passed on by infected body fluids – semen, blood and the secretions from a woman's vagina.

Groups at high risk from AIDS are:

- *Homosexual* or *bisexual* people who are sexually active (see pp. 111-112).
- *Drug-abusers* who share used needles which may have infected blood on them.
- *Babies* conceived by mothers who are infected.
- *Heterosexual* people who are in *intimate* sexual contact with infected persons. (*Heterosexual* refers to people who are attracted to the opposite sex, as most people are.)
- *Haemophiliacs* (people with a blood condition who require regular blood transfusions) are most at risk in countries where blood-screening facilities are inadequate. Blood for transfusion is carefully screened in this country.
- The sexual partners of any of those listed above.

There is no known cure for HIV / AIDS. However, the virus is not passed on in any way other than those listed above. It cannot be caught by casual contact, e.g. handshaking or hugging. Nor can it be caught from utensils or drinking vessels; from food or water; from toilets, washing or swimming facilities, or from soiled clothes or bed-linen. Nor can sneezing, coughing or spitting spread this infection.

Avoiding AIDS

- If you *abstain from sexual intercourse* except with one faithful partner (who is also faithful to you).

and

- If you *do not become involved in drug abuse –* injecting drugs.

THEN YOU WILL NOT CONTRACT HIV/AIDS

So we *do know how to avoid* this fatal illness.

Condoms cannot give 100 per cent protection against HIV/AIDS. In fact condoms are less effective against the HIV virus than against pregnancy because the HIV virus is 450 times smaller than sperm and can therefore penetrate the tiny inherent flaws in particular condoms.

So, though condom use is advocated in prevention against AIDS, some experts say that promotion of condoms for that purpose 'is dangerous and irresponsible' (see C. M. Roland, 'Rubber Chemistry and Technology', *Sunday Record*, 24 January 1993).

In the main cities of Ireland there are clinics where simple blood tests can be done to ascertain if a person has a STD or HIV infection. Your family doctor will refer you for the test.

> Doesn't it become more and more clear why moral living is the best? God, the Creator, knows all the pain and wants to keep us safe.

QUESTIONS YOU MAY WONDER ABOUT

(All the following questions have been asked countless times by adolescents. So here's your chance to get some ready-made answers. But don't hesitate to discuss any questions or answers with which you have further difficulty.)

Q. It's hard to talk about sex with anyone at home. What can I do?

A. Tell your parents that you'd love to talk. Perhaps have a list of things you'd like to discuss. Share this book with them. Reading it together can lead to great chats. Parents may be shy or think that you are not yet ready for such discussions. So do let them know.

Q. I have only one parent at home. How can I tell my friends because they all have two?

A. Just tell it simply like it is. Nowadays parents separate for various reasons and people understand that this can happen. Be open and not defensive. That's life, and the parent you have at home loves you and would, I'm sure, like to meet your pals.

Q. I'm thirteen. Is it a sin to kiss my boyfriend?

A. Sin is always unloving and uncaring of what is best for yourself and the other person. What feels nice is not always what is best. I advise you to keep the kisses occasional and light. Kisses have a way of increasing and multiplying rapidly! So do be careful. Enjoy other things in the friendship.

Q. How does a baby become a boy baby or a girl baby?

A. To put it simply, each sperm is either male or female. Whichever one reaches the mother's egg first causes the baby to be a girl baby or a boy baby. The egg is neutral.

Q. If you don't get off with someone you fancy your pals will jeer you and tell everyone. What can you do?

A. Have the courage to smile and say 'I'm waiting for the right time'. It is *your* friendship and you and the person you fancy should decide how *you two* want it to be. Don't forget, anyone is able to French kiss. The more intelligent ones build a friendship first. Be cool and light-hearted when your pals try to tease you. Don't let it get to you. Lots of adolescents prefer not to kiss yet.

Q. Should a fellow and girl marry if she gets pregnant when they are going together?

A. It would be a great mistake to rush into marriage in that situation. The boy should stand by his girlfriend and help her in any way he can. Later, after the baby is born, the friendship may continue and grow into true love. Or it may not.

Q. Why do some people marry in a registry office?

A. They do so in order to make their commitment to one another legal and formal. They do not seek the blessing of the Church.

Q. People often dare you to drink alcohol from supermarkets. What can I say to get out of taking it?

A. Well, underage drinking is illegal. The habit of over-indulging in alcohol can begin very early for show-offs. Many of them will become pot-bellied, will risk getting ulcers, damaging their livers, brains, kidneys and hearts. They'll be no good at sports if they become dependent on alcohol. Aren't those enough reasons for keeping away from it?

Q. **How can I get my Dad to stop smoking? I'm afraid he'll die before he's old.**

A. The best you can do is tell him of your very real fear. We're told that every cigarette shortens the smokers life by 10-15 minutes. But 10 years after giving up the smokes his system should be pretty healthy again. Suggest that he try the various helps available. Even chewing gum can help. The doctor may be able to advise your Dad about therapy. But the bottom line is that it is your Dad himself who must make the decision. Keep encouraging whatever effort he makes. And don't be tempted to start smoking yourself.

Q. **What is rape?**

A. Rape means forcing a person to have sexual intercourse. It is a violent crime. Avoid taking lifts from strangers who may abuse or rape you. And don't travel home at night by yourself, or take short-cuts down lanes when it's dark. Most people are ordinary and nice. But don't chance meeting the oddbod who may abuse you. Take sensible care.

Q. **Could a girl get pregnant if she was raped?**

A. Yes, she could if she were fertile at the time of the rape. The girl should report the matter immediately to the police and go straight to a hospital out-patients to have the semen washed out of her uterus.

Q. **What do 'riding', 'screwing' and 'laying' mean?**

A. They are degrading and vulgar terms for love-making and sexual intercourse.

Q. **What is a virgin?**

A. A virgin is a person (male or female) who has not had sexual intercourse. Mary, Jesus' mother, conceived him without having sexual intercourse. God the Father caused the ovum within Mary to be fertilised miraculously. Joseph became the foster-father.

Q.   What is an orgy?
A.   An orgy is a party at which there is an excessive indulgence in drink or sex or drugs.

Q.   What is an orgasm?
A.   It is the name for the climax of excitement in sexual intercourse.

Q.   Is it normal for a girl to have a whitish discharge from the vagina even before her first period?
A.   Yes, that is quite normal. The glands in the lining of the vagina produce a healthy cleansing and lubricating fluid.

Q.   What is a 'section' birth?
A.   The full name for it is Caesarean Section. It is when the normal birth procedure isn't advisable or possible. The mother is given an anaesthetic and the baby is taken from the womb through an incision in the mother's stomach. It is a fairly commonplace operation and a mother may have more than one baby in this way.

Q.   How can I tell my mum that I've got my periods?
A.   Your mother will know that you are due to get periods like every adolescent girl. So all you need say is 'Mum, my periods have arrived.'

Q.   What is oral sex (or 'blow job' or 'rainbow kiss')?
A.   Oral sex is applying the mouth to another person's sexual organs. This is never right for unmarried

people. Married people make personal decisions about it. Do remember that sexual diseases can be transmitted in this way.

Q. What is child abuse?
A. It is when an adult abuses a child by improper touches or actions, by violence, hitting or abusive language.

Q. If an adult touches a child's sexual parts, what is the right thing to do?
A. Tell a responsible grown-up right away. Keep your distance from the abusing adult and say a clear 'NO' if that person tries to touch you that way again. If necessary phone Childline (Freephone 1800 666 666), who will advise you what to do.

Q. If only one sperm is enough to cause a baby to be conceived, where do all the others go after intercourse?
A. The rest of the sperm disintegrate in the body and pass from the body unnoticed.

Q. I'm twelve and don't really want a boyfriend. Is that normal?
A. Very usual and normal. Sometimes you get the impression that all your classmates have boyfriends but they certainly have not. They may just talk about boys. Be yourself and don't rush.

Q. What does 'frigid' mean?
A. 'Frigid' in this context means cold and unresponsive. If a woman is not responsive it is often because she is not attracted to that particular man. If a fellow asks you 'Are you frigid?' say 'No, just choosy'. (Many

adolescent boys don't know what frigid means. They just think it's smart to say.)

Q. **If a girl says you're 'no good' what can you do?**
A. Laugh it off and say 'I'm very good with the right person'.

Q. **What is incest?**
A. It is having sex with a member of one's own family (including a close relative). It is wrong medically and morally.

Q. **If a boy and a girl nearly have sex, can she get pregnant?**
A. The two would need to have removed their clothes. If the penis places the semen near the opening of the vagina, a sperm could travel in and pregnancy could result.

Q. **Should we be allowed to go to discos at twelve?**
A. I would be slow to allow twelve-year-olds go to discos.

Q. **What is a foetus or an embryo?**
A. An embryo is the technical word for the newly conceived baby until the beginning of the third month of pregnancy. From then until birth it is called a foetus.

Q. **If grown men use bad language, why not us?**
A. 'Grown' doesn't always mean 'mature'. Some people haven't shaken off their youthful bad habits. So try to give them a good example.

Q. **What does 'genitals' mean?**
A. The genitals are the male and female sex organs.

Q. **What do 'wank', 'toss', 'frig' mean?**

A. They are vulgar words for masturbation. (See p. 61.)

Q. **I'd hate to go to a disco. Am I normal?**

A. Yes, of course you are normal. Even many much older teenagers dislike the disco scene. Everyone has their own likes and dislikes.

Q. **Dad and Mum sometimes have awful fights and I'm afraid. What can I do?**

A. When all is quiet again tell one or both of your parents how afraid and worried you are. They may not realise.

Q. **What are test-tube babies? (IVF)**

A. A test-tube baby is created in laboratory conditions by extracting semen from the father and ova (eggs) from the mother and putting these together in a glass container. This container is kept at the same temperature as a woman's womb would be. If and when an ovum is fertilised by a sperm in the container, a new human being is present in embryo. The embryo is then inserted into the mother's womb in the hope that it will plant itself and develop normally. In fact this is successful in only about one in three attempts. This procedure is called in vitro fertilisation (IVF).

A moral problem arises if more than one ovum is fertilised in the glass container because usually the strongest embryo is chosen to insert into the mother's womb. Then, if other conceptions have taken place in the container, a moral problem arises if these are destroyed. Often IVF fails and no conception results.

Q. Why would a couple want to have test-tube babies?

A. If, for some medical reason, the couple have been unable to conceive a baby in the normal way they might look into the possibility of IVF.

Q. What is a surrogate mother?

A. A surrogate mother is a substitute mother. When, for medical reasons, a woman is unable to conceive or nurture a baby in her womb the test-tube method (as above) is tried. If a conception takes place in the test tube the foetus is put into another woman's womb to be developed. (The parents would have selected the woman to take over the pregnancy.) Surrogacy can cause many legal problems. It removes the baby's right to be bonded to its mother during pregnancy and the surrogate mother may argue that it is bonded with her and is, therefore, hers.

Q. What is a hysterectomy operation? My Mum had one. Will she be okay?

A. A hysterectomy is the removal of the uterus (womb) if it has become unhealthy. Many women have this operation and recover well from it. Of course, once the womb is removed a woman cannot have another baby. Give your Mum plenty of help so that she will take things easy for the weeks following the operation. She will tend to tire easily but will regain her strength as the months go by.

Q. What does 'gay' mean?

A. 'Gay' is the name often used for a homosexual person. Gay people are sexually attracted to members of their own sex. Lesbians are gay women.

(Remember, heterosexual is the word used to describe

the majority of people who are attracted to members of the opposite sex).

Q. **If a person is bisexual, what does that mean?**

A. Bisexual is a word used to describe adults who are sexually attracted to both males and females. It is not understood why a minority of people become gay or bisexual though some studies indicate that there are either biological or psychological reasons.

It is not wrong to be homosexual (gay). Homosexual people must behave in a morally responsible way. It is wrong for them to try to influence adversely the development of adolescents or others.

In spite of their sexual disadvantage, homosexual people can achieve success in any aspect of life or chosen career, just like anyone else. It is wrong to use mocking names (such as 'homo', 'queer', 'bent', 'fairy', 'lessie', etc.) to describe a gay person or to show rejection or prejudice towards such a person.

Q. **If a person has a crush on someone of his or her own sex, is he or she homosexual?**

A. Some adolescents experience a great attraction or natural admiration for a member of their own sex. This is often called 'a crush' and is different from true homosexuality which is felt by some adults. Especially during puberty, when emotions are still getting sorted out, homosexual feeling may be felt. Just do not act on such passing feelings. A young person who is worried by such mixed-up feelings should chat to a parent, doctor or therapist.

STORIES FOR DISCUSSION AND ROLE PLAY

Anne and John's Story

Anne is a 6th Class primary school girl. She is twelve. John was in the same school – a class above her until last year. Now he is in the college in First Year. They live quite close to one another. They played together with the other kids as they were growing up.

A number of the girls in Anne's class are talking and giggling about the lads they 'fancy'. Anne feels that they all have boyfriends, that she is the only one without one. She joins in the gossip and laughs. She doesn't want to appear uncool and childish, to be left out, called names and jeered at. Anne doesn't really know about some of the apparently rude words and activities which send the other girls into smothered laughter and whispers, but she laughs too.

One day Anne stopped to talk to John on the way home. It was about his cousins who used to live on the road until the family went to England. Now they have returned.

As they spoke some of Anne's classmates passed. They shouted: 'Hi Anne!' in that special tone. They passed on, laughing and nudging each other. John reddened and hurried on. Did he like her? she wondered. Did I blush? she asked herself, feeling silly and childish.

Next day in school there was a note scrawled inside her jotter reading 'Do you fancy him, Anne?' She put the jotter away quickly and her heart beat in an unexpected way. There was a snort of laughter from behind. She turned around and saw some of the girls whispering. One asked 'Are you feeling hot, Anne?' more laughter. At breaktime they asked 'Are you going with John Carter?' 'Why didn't you tell us?' 'Did he ask you to go with him?' 'What did you say?' 'Will you get off with him?' Anne tried to tell them that John was just a friend. But part of her began to feel that maybe he was more than that. Suddenly he seemed to be a different person and she felt something change in herself. She didn't really want to go with fellas yet. But now she felt she had to. The teasing didn't stop. She wondered if John might fancy her too. How would she know? she asked herself. Supposing he asked her out, what would she do? 'Mum would blow a fuse if she knew', Anne decided. Or if he asked her to go with him and she was expected to 'get off' with him she wouldn't know how to do it properly. Yet she'd have to, in case he told others that she was 'tight' or 'frigid', as other girls had been told.

She couldn't ask her Mum. They never talked about things like that. Part of her wished she could. She felt worried and preoccupied by thoughts of things she had heard and read about – babies outside marriage and condoms and rape. In bed she wept. I must be the only one who doesn't know. She began to go to school the long way, by the park, avoiding the road John lived on. But one day he came out of the park, kicking a ball with his pals. Anne felt herself blush but she called over 'Hi, John!' He looked the other way and ran past. Anne heard the lads laugh. One called to her 'D'ye fancy our Johnnie?' More laughter. Anne didn't turn around but tears pricked her eyes. She ran home and banged the kitchen door, not answering her mother's greetings. She ran into the bathroom and locked the door. She felt like a stranger to herself, fed-up, worried, yet with some sort of excited feeling. She looked in the mirror and saw a shiny face and crooked teeth. 'I'm awful', she groaned.

After Anne had passed by, John felt the fun had gone out of

the afternoon. His pals started questioning him. 'You never told us, are you going with her?' 'Did you have it off yet?' 'Wow! look at lover boy...'. 'She just lives there', John growled. 'She just lives there', they mimicked, mincing along in front of him making kissing sounds. Reaching home, John made for the door as casually as he could. 'Bye, lover boy', shouted the lads. John didn't turn around but he heard their laughter. He raced up to his room and put on some loud music in case someone called him. He felt that he had to be alone.

'What did it all mean?' John wondered. 'Does she fancy me?' What did she expect him to do? How would he go about doing that? Oh, no! Would she expect him to do those kisses, a Frenchie! He'd never shifted anyone before. Other lads had; maybe they ALL had, judging by their talk. Would she laugh? But if she didn't she might tell the other girls. The lads might hear. John could almost hear them say, as they had of Danno, 'A date and not getting off, he must be gay'. John had joined in the laughter over Danno... did he fancy Anne? He wasn't sure what the feeling would be. She was friendly so maybe he should say he fancied her. Would he phone her and say it? How would he actually get around to saying it? She might tell him to get lost. Three times he went to the phone, hesitated and went back upstairs in an anguish of indecision. His Dad called up, 'Will you settle down to your homework and stop all the running around.' John muttered something under his breath and banged his bedroom door.

Around the corner, in the avenue, Anne left her bedroom door open a bit. The phone might ring. It might, just possibly, be him. She had butterflies in her stomach for some reason. When ten o'clock came she knew he wouldn't phone. How she hated the way her teeth were and her hair.

She thought, 'I'll never get a boyfriend. And now I haven't even got a boy who is a friend. The misery of it,' she sobbed into her pillow.

* * * * *

Friendship Stories: For discussion and decisions
Carrie and Anna had been friends since they were in 2nd Class. They lived quite close to each other, played together and shared secrets.

In September of 5th Class a new girl came into their school. Linda was pretty and good fun. Soon Carrie began to chat to her and join her at break. Linda was daring and thought of all sorts of new things to do.

One Saturday Carrie phoned Anna and said that she couldn't go with her to the shopping centre because her mum wanted her for something. Anna was disappointed but she went shopping with her mother in Roches. She was delighted when her mum suggested that they have a snack in the café there. But her delight didn't last long because across at the other side of the café she saw Carrie's red head, and with her was Linda, laughing and enjoying ice creams together.

Anna felt her face go red and tears pricked her eyes. She moved her chair a little so that the other two couldn't see her. Suddenly her cream cake tasted like sawdust. Her mum noticed. 'Are you feeling okay?' she asked. Anna said she felt a bit sick. So they left the café to go out in the air.

That evening Anna wanted to telephone Carrie but she couldn't. She was afraid she might cry on the phone. She raged inside herself thinking 'She **lied** to me. She doesn't want to be my friend. I've no best friend now. I thought I could **trust** her. I feel so **lonely**.' She sobbed as she tried to go to sleep.

On Monday at school, Anna and Carrie sat in their usual places. (The teacher didn't allow places to be changed.) 'Hi', said Carrie brightly. Anna pretended to be busy getting out her books. She didn't reply. She paid great attention to the teacher, never glancing at Carrie. 'What's up?' asked Carrie after class. 'You should know 'what's up',' said Anna angrily. 'You're a b…. You lied to me about Saturday.' She saw that Carrie was taken aback. Carrie responded, 'Well, Linda invited me. Is that a sin?' 'There was no need to lie', said Anna, stalking away in case Carrie noticed tears coming to her eyes. She went into the toilet.

At break Linda and Carrie sat on the wall sharing their lunch and laughing. Anna tried to join with other girls and they asked, 'What's wrong with you and Carrie?' Anna said airily 'You couldn't trust her', adding, 'Anyway, Mum doesn't like her'. 'Why?' asked Mary. 'Because she's too big for her boots. Carrying on in town and all that', said Anna. Her anger and hurt made her want to hit out at Carrie. The bell went.

As they filed back to class Mary edged over to Carrie. 'So what were you up to?' she asked smirking. 'How do you mean?' asked Carrie. 'Oh I've heard things about you', said Mary. Liz joined in. 'Yes. What way were you 'carrying on'?' Linda turned to Carrie. 'That's Anna's lies. She's **jealous**.' They laughed.

What next? Can things be made good? How?

* * * * *

117

Brian's mistake

Brian's Dad is well-off. For Christmas Brian got a three-in-one music system. He and his pals, Tom and Conor, decided to try to produce a few tapes. Brian knew a fair bit about tape-producing and was a bit bossy.

Conor had really good ideas about how they could do it. He was very keen on mechanical things. He spent a lot of time at home working out plans for the project. Tom often dropped in to help him and they brought their ideas and equipment to Brian's place. Brian took it all over as though he had thought it all up. He lorded it over them and asked his Dad to get some more equipment.

Even though Tom and Conor felt a bit jealous of Brian they also got a bit fed-up with him. Before Easter Tom and Conor took on Saturday jobs. They planned to save up for a second-hand music system like Brian's.

By the summer they had enough money to get the system. They had learnt a lot more about tape-production in the time spent with Brian. So what did they do? They dumped Brian and got together to work on their new plans. Brian found himself alone. It was no fun doing it alone. He had lost his mates. *They never bothered about him now.*

Exercise

Role-play a scene where the three lads are working on the project. What did Brian do to annoy his pals? What could he have done to keep the group together? Could he have listened better, paced himself to them? Is there anything Brian can do now? Should Tom and Conor have behaved differently?

* * * * *

Hallowe'en Story

At Hallowe'en 6 or 8 lads of 10 to 12 years of age lit a bonfire.

Nearby were derelict houses where stray cats roamed. They caught one of the cats and put it in a box.

At the height of the fire they threw the box into the flames to see what would happen.

A couple of older lads were passing and heard the cat. They quickly realised what the younger lads had done. One of them grabbed a branch of a tree that hadn't yet been thrown onto the fire. He poked the box which was still flaming and knocked it off the fire.

The dazed cat limped out. The older boys turned on the younger ones with the same tree branch. 'You need a wallop of this', they said. But the young boys raced off and got away.

Discuss

What do you think about what happened?
Why did the younger boys do such a cruel thing?
Would you have joined in with them?
If you were the older lads, would you have acted as they did or differently?

GOD'S WORD

We sometimes hear about God's Word but we may never have realised how comforting and loving his words can be. And his promises last for ever. Just listen to the following phrases from the Old and New Testaments and hear them as though God is whispering them in your ear today. For God did not speak these words to one generation only. I just love to realise that when I read what he has said; it is as though he is saying these warm words to me personally. He is eternally faithful, forgiving and understanding. Now listen:

'You are mine … You are precious in my eyes, you are honoured and I love you.' (Isaiah 43:1-4)

'Don't be afraid or discouraged for I, the Lord your God, am with you wherever you go' (Joshua 1:9).

'I will not forget you. Behold I have carved you on the palms of my hands.' (Isaiah 49:15-17)

'Peace I leave with you. My peace I give unto you.' (John 14:27)

'I have loved you with an everlasting love.' (Jeremiah 31:3)

'Your heavenly Father knows what you need.' (Matthew 6:32)

'My grace is sufficient for you for my power is greatest when you are weak.' (2 Cor 12:7-10)

'How often have I longed to gather you under my wings as a hen gathers her chicks, and you refused.' (Matthew 23:37)

'Look, I am standing at the door knocking.' (Rev 3:20)

Jesus said to the twelve 'What about you? Do you want to go away too?' Simon Peter said 'Who shall we go to? You have the words of eternal life.' (John 6:67)

'You are home. It is all I have ever wanted.' (The father to the prodigal son.)

'You must come away to some lonely place all by yourself and rest for a while.' (Mark 6:31)

'I bless you, Father, Lord of heaven and earth, for hiding these things from the learned and the clever and revealing them to mere children.' (Luke 10:21-22)

A Favourite Prayer
TO JESUS, MY FRIEND

by
Blessed Claude de la Colombière SJ

O Jesus! You are my true friend, my only friend. You take part in all my misfortunes; you take them on yourself; you know how to change them into blessings.
You listen to me with the greatest kindness when I relate my troubles to you, and you have always balm to pour on my wounds.

I find you at all times, I find you everywhere, you never go away; if I have to change my dwelling, I find you there wherever I go.

You are never weary of listening to me, you are never tired of doing me good.

I am certain of being loved by you, if I love you; my goods are nothing to you, and by bestowing yours on me, you never grow poor. However miserable I may be, no one more noble or clever or even holier can come between you and me, and deprive me of your friendship; and death, which tears us away from all other friends, will unite me forever to you.

All the humiliations attached to old age or to the loss of honour will never detach you from me; on the contrary, I shall never enjoy you more fully, and you will never be closer to me than when everything seems to conspire against me, to overwhelm me, and to cast me down.

You bear with all my faults with extreme patience and even my want of fidelity and my ingratitude do not wound you to such a degree as to make you unwilling to receive me back when I return to you.

Jesus, grant that I may die praising you, that I may die loving you and that I may die for love of you.

A BASIC RESOURCE LIST FOR PARENTS OF PRIMARY SCHOOL CHILDREN

Books

Becoming a Man,
William Bausch, 23rd Publications, 1988

Becoming a Woman
Valerie Vance Dillon, Columba Press, 1990

Boyfacts & Girlfacts
Peter Bird & Cathy Bee, ed. Aidan Herron, Poolbeg Press, 1995

Boy Talk
Lucienne Pickering, Continuum, 1992

Bringing Up Responsible Teenagers
John Sharry, Veritas Publications, 2001

Coping with Bullying in Schools,
Brendan Byrne, Continuum, 1994

Girl Talk
Lucienne Pickering, Continuum, 1992

Parenting in the New Millenium — 17 Expert Opinions
Louis Power, ed., Nurture, 2000

Rite of Passage: How to Teach your Son about Sex and Manhood
E. James Wilder, Vine Books, Servant Publications, 1994

The Way We Live Now
Maureen Gaffney, Gill & Macmillan, 1996

Who Made Me? (for very young children)
Malcolm and Meryl Doney, Marshall Pickering, 1992

Books by Michael and Terri Quinn:
What Can the Parents of a Teenager Do?
Taking Charge of your Life – Assertiveness,
Family Caring, 1988

Books from the *Will Our Children Be Okay?* series:
Bringing Up Responsible Children
John Sharry, Veritas Publications, 1999

Children Feeling Good
Tony Humphries, Veritas Publications, 1998

Helping Your Child Through Bereavement
Mary Paula Walsh, Veritas Publications, 2000

How Will Our Children Grow?
Christy Kenneally, Veritas Publications, 1998

When Parents Separate: Helping Your Children Cope
John Sharry, Peter Reid, Eugene Donohoe, Veritas
Publications, 2001

Will Our Children Believe?
M. P. Gallagher SJ, Veritas Publications, 1998

Will Our Children Build Healthy Relationships?
Angela Macnamara, Veritas Publications, 1999

Will Our Children Have Family Prayer?
Clare Moloney, Veritas Publications, 1999

Your Child and Drugs
Sean Cassin, Veritas Publications, 1999

Videos
Sex Education for Girls (10-12-year-olds)
Angela Macnamara, Veritas

Sex Education for Boys (10-12-year-olds)
Angela Macnamara & Francis McCrickard, Veritas

HELPING AGENCIES

Childline Freephone 1800 666 666
Helpline for children who are in difficulty. There is no need to give your full name.

ONE2ONE
Drugs and sexual health helpline especially for young people
Cork Tel (021) 427 5615

AIDS ALLIANCE
Confidential telephone support and information service
Dublin Tel (01) 873 4277 Mon-Fri 7.00-9.00 pm Sat 3.00-5.00 pm
Cork Tel (021) 427 6676 Mon-Fri 10.00 am-5.00 pm
Galway Tel (091) 562213

Al Anon (AA) Family groups (see telephone directory)
Help for families of alcoholics
5/6 Capel Street, Dublin 1 Tel (01) 873 2699 Mon-Sat 10.30 am-2.30 pm

Alateen To help young people whose lives have been upset by a parent's compulsive drinking.
5/6 Capel Street, Dublin 1 Tel (01) 873 2699 Mon-Sat 10.30 am-2.30 pm

Steps Youth Advice and Counselling Service
30/31 Bride Street, Dublin 2 Tel (01) 473 4143
40 Abbey Street, Wexford Tel (053) 238646
12 Mary Street, Cork Tel (021) 496 2949
22 Thomas Street, Limerick Tel (061) 400 088
37 George's Street, Waterford Tel (051) 304476
Run by ISPCC to give young people a chance to talk about growing up, relationships, alcohol, drugs, child abuse, bereavement, etc.

Irish Allergy Association PO Box 1067, Churchtown, Dublin 14

Asthma Society of Ireland Information and advice service
15-17 Eden Quay, Dublin 1 Tel (01) 878 8511.
AsthmaLine Callsave 1850 445464. Local Branches.

Irish Society for Prevention of Cruelty to Children (ISPCC)
20 Molesworth Street, Dublin 2 Tel (01) 679 4944 10.00 am-10.00 pm

Bullying – National Association for victims of
Frederick Street, Clara, Co Offaly Tel (0506) 31590
Supports and advises children, families and teachers. Counselling by
telephone or in private.

Campaign Against Bullying
72 Lakelands Avenue, Stillorgan, Co. Dublin Tel (01) 288 7976

Barnardos National Childrens' Resource Centre
Block 4, Christ Church Square, Dublin 8 Tel (01) 454 9699
Services for young people in need and their families.

Parent to Parent
Carmichael House, North Brunswick Street Tel (01) 872 5550
Helpline for parents of children with special needs (e.g. mental or
physical disability, blindness, etc.).

Aware Helping to defeat depression
Helpline (01) 679 1711 Mon-Fri 10.00 am-4.00 pm and 6.00-10.00 pm
Assists and supports those suffering from mood disorder and their
families. Support groups in 25 towns.

Samaritans See your local telephone directory for branches in your area.
112 Marlborough Street, Dublin 1 Tel (01) 872 7700
Befriends the lonely, despairing and suicidal.
Special reduced rate telephone line (11p) 1850 609 090

Parentline Tel (01) 873 3500
Anonymous telephone listening service for parents under stress.

Gamblers Anonymous Answering Service (01) 872 1133
For those who desire to stop compulsive gambling.

Overeaters Anonymous
PO Box 2529, Dublin 5 Tel (01) 451 5138
Self-help for those suffering from eating disorders.

ACCORD Catholic Marriage Counselling Service
All Hallows, Dublin 9 Tel (01) 837 1151 (over 50 centres nationwide)
For those experiencing difficulties in their relationships

Marriage Counselling Service
24 Grafton Street, Dublin 2 Tel (01) 679 9341
Marriage counselling, mediation, schools' education service.

Cherish
2 Lower Pembroke Street, Dublin 2 Tel (01) 662 9212
Single parents association. Non-directive counselling. Practical assistance.

CURA (see your local telephone directory for branches in your area.)
30 South Anne Street, Dublin 2 Tel (01) 671 0598
Counselling and practical help for women and girls with unplanned pregnancies. Foster care, adoption counselling, post-natal care.

Rape Crisis Centre
70 Lower Leeson Street, Dublin 2 Tel (01) 661 4911
Freephone 1800 778 888 for 24-hour counselling
26 McCurtain Street, Cork Freephone 1800 496 496

Focus Point
14a Eustace Street, Dublin 2 Tel (01) 671 2555
For people with severe accommodation problems.